The publication of
On the Edge of Splendor:
Exploring Grand Canyon's Human Past
was supported by generous contributions from:

Charlotte N. Gray
The Inn at Loretto in Santa Fe
The National Geographic Society
J. Michael and Marianne O'Shaughnessy
Grand Canyon Natural History Association

On the Edge of Splendor:

Exploring Grand Canyon's Human Past

Douglas W. Schwartz

EXPLORATION
Annual Bulletin of the School of American Research

David Grant Noble, Series Editor
Tom Ireland,   Editor
Deborah Flynn Post,   Art Director
Willow Powers, Picture Researcher

Contents

Acknowledgments

A scholar's work always benefits from the advice and thought of others. In all of my previous articles and monographs on Grand Canyon archaeology I have acknowledged the help of many people — crew members, colleagues, financial contributors, supporting organizations, and always the critical cooperation of staff members of Grand Canyon National Park. The essays in this volume were significantly enriched by the help of the following individuals: Thomas Cartledge, Jeffrey Dean, Fred Eggan, Richard Emerick, Robert Euler, Leanne Hinton, Lisa Inkret, Tom Ireland, Calvin Jennings, Joann Kealinohomoku, Robert Kelly, Jerrold Levy, Dan Murphy, David Noble, Albert Schroeder, Alan Sullivan, and Barton Wright. Of course I am responsible for any shortcomings that may occur here.

Douglas W. Schwartz
President, School of American Research

Chapter I

The Grand Canyon. Photo by John MacGregor, 1968. School of American Research.

Beginnings in Wonder and Curiosity

Reaching the edge of the canyon on a hot June day in 1949, I was overwhelmed by what lay before me: a bedrock gorge of tremendous magnitude in depth and breadth; a rainbow of soft colors; a confusion of shapes; and a harsh ruggedness, all of which combined into a powerful image of natural splendor. Then as my mind and eyes gradually moved back from the scope of this geological apparition, I began to comprehend some of its details. The rift before me was not only miles wide, but it stretched as far as I could see to the east and west. As the haze of the early morning lightened, outlines emerged deep below — mesas and valleys larger than any I had ever seen, yet here, only aspects of a vast natural complex unique in the world. I was seeing, for the first time, the Grand Canyon of the Colorado River. It would be years before it became apparent that on that day my life changed forever.

Years later I found a quotation by the naturalist John Muir that expressed my feelings precisely: "No matter how far you have wandered . . . or how many famous gorges and valleys you have seen, this one, the Grand Canyon of the Colorado, will seem . . . as unearthly in color and grandeur and quality of architecture as if you had found it on some other star."

Later that morning, as I hiked down the Kaibab Trail, the vastness and beauty of the canyon became increasingly apparent, and its special mystery took hold of my imagination. I was full of questions about the canyon's origin, biology, and human history. Suddenly, I wanted to learn all there was to know about this special place.

At the time, I was an undergraduate student working thirty miles south of the Grand Canyon on an archaeological field project sponsored by the University of Illinois and the Museum of Northern Arizona, a position that gave me an opportunity to learn more about the Grand Canyon from the national park rangers, the specialists on our excavation team, and the museum scientists. To my amazement (I was twenty and very susceptible to amazement), I found that while a great deal was known about the geology and biology of the Grand Canyon, the history of its inhabitants before the arrival of Europeans was largely a mystery. Some "ancient ruins" were present, small collections of old pottery and stone artifacts had been made, and petroglyphs had been observed on remote canyon walls, but no systematic work had been carried out within the canyon. On the plateaus above, only three surveys and one excavation had been conducted — hardly what I had expected for a canyon 15 miles wide and, within the national park, nearly 300 miles long and bordered by hundreds of thousands of square miles of forested plateau to the north and south. But the random observations of former visitors and the results of the four isolated projects were all I needed to whet my curiosity. Here was a scientific adventure offering itself to me, with places to explore and new answers to seek. This experience was the beginning of a life's work, gradually leading me, not to the discovery of a prehistoric people in the canyon, but to a whole pageant of unique ways of life.

Over the next four years, while I was completing my undergraduate work at the University of Kentucky and beginning my doctoral studies at Yale, always, in the back of my mind, burned a fascination with the Grand Canyon. Who were the early settlers of the region? When did they arrive, and where had they come from? How did they live in that harsh environment, and what role did the canyon play in shaping their lives? Why did they leave, and where did they go? Eventually, but years later, I also began to wonder how the Grand Canyon's effect on its settlers compared to that of the world's many other harsh, out-of-the-way places on their human inhabitants.

In 1953 I returned to the canyon to conduct research for my doctoral dissertation on the prehistory of the Havasupais, the one group of American Indians who continue to live within the Grand Canyon. Then, following the completion of that work and after I started teaching at the University of Kentucky, I began a systematic program of archaeological research in the canyon that lasted for over twenty years, excavating in caves in the inner canyon and surveying in side canyons and along the Colorado River. In the summer of 1967, I began four seasons of major excavations within the canyon, but also on Unkar and Bright Angel deltas and on the North Rim in the area of the Walhalla Plateau, for after all this time there still had been no new excavations within the canyon or any new work on its ruins. Finally, after the completion of some ten projects, I began to feel enough information was available to begin to answer some of my original questions, while, of course, new ones were already forming in my mind.

During these two decades and since that time, other archaeologists have also been working in the Grand Canyon region, adding to our understanding of its prehistory: John McGregor from the University of Illinois, whom I first worked for as an undergraduate; Joe Ben Wheat from the University of Colorado; Alan Sullivan of the University of Arizona; Robert Euler and Trinkle Jones of the National Park Service; Richard Effland; Peter Pilles from the Museum of Northern Arizona; and Thomas Cartledge of the United States Forest Service. Our work and that of others has created a pool of information, not all of it in agreement, but enough so to begin to construct the outline and some intriguing details of prehistoric life in the area of the Grand Canyon.

This issue of Exploration *synthesizes the results of that work, beginning with the contribution of the canyon's extraordinary early explorer, John Wesley Powell, the first white man who observed archaeological remains there. Powell's initial conclusions about Grand Canyon prehistory, based on the scraps of information he collected, were far simpler than the story that can be pieced together today. But that is the nature of scientific progress, and the conclusions we make today will certainly be added to and improved upon by future generations of archaeological work.*

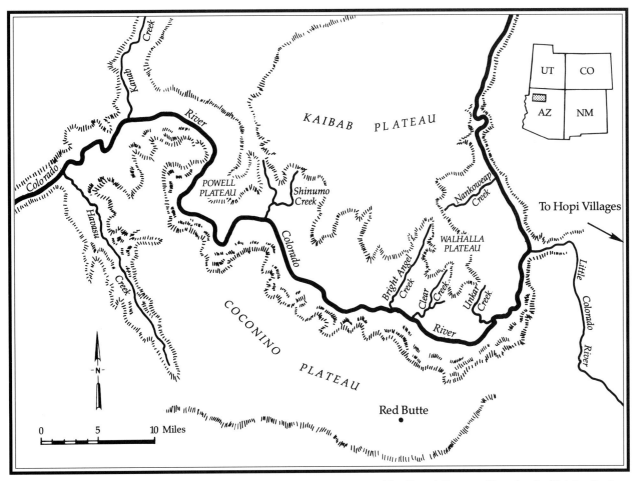

The Grand Canyon. Drawing by Katrina Lasko.

Chapter II

"Running a Rapid." Illustration for John Wesley Powell's *Report on the Exploration of the Colorado River*.

What Powell Discovered

The Colorado River surged through the Grand Canyon in a more powerful and dangerous torrent than John Wesley Powell had ever imagined it could. When he began his great adventure of exploration in 1869, he knew he would face the unexpected, but he had not counted on the awesome power of the river, its treacherous whirlpools, the frightening roar as it billowed over the huge boulders hidden just below the surface, or the strength of its man-killing rapids. The cliffs above the river were higher by far than he had thought possible, in places reaching out of sight, shortening the days by blocking the early morning and late afternoon sun, forming a barrier that made escape seem impossible.

Well into the journey, his crew became increasingly anxious as they approached every new rapid or bend in the river. In earlier disastrous dunkings they had lost precious food to the muddy waters and had been thrown from their boats after colliding violently with boulders that cracked the sturdy wooden crafts like twigs. And always, buried not too deeply in their minds, were speculations heard before they embarked that somewhere in the unexplored canyon the river could sink into the middle of the earth and they would never be seen or heard from again. However, throughout the voyage, Powell was convinced that they could safely complete their scientific mission to explore the river and observe its wonders: the rocks, the river's course, the plants, the animals, and any evidence that other humans had preceded them within these fascinating depths.

John Wesley Powell was an exceptional man of driving ambition who had already overcome much more than he thought the river might deliver. Born in 1834, he had grown up on small midwestern farms and developed an early interest in natural history. To make a living he began teaching, but his passion was long river trips such as one he took down the Mississippi from St. Paul to New Orleans. During the Civil War, he became a commander in the Illinois Artillery and was critically wounded at the battle of Shiloh, losing his right arm. After the war he taught courses in botany, zoology, anatomy, entomology, and geology at Illinois Wesleyan College.

Powell also had a deep interest in the West and the exploration of the Rockies. As William H. Goetzmann wrote in *Exploration and Empire*, Powell's first expedition was intended "to explore the Upper Colorado River and solve the mysteries of its three hundred mile canyon," thereby shedding light on "the central forces that formed the continent." This goal led to the daring proposal to descend the 1,500 miles of unexplored Colorado River, including the Grand Canyon — "the climactic event of late-nineteenth-century exploration" and "the opening up of the last completely unknown territory in the continental United States."

Following his canyon adventure, only a small part of which I relate below, Powell went on to become the founder of the Bureau of

American Ethnology and, later, director of the U.S. Geological Survey. Yet whatever his other accomplishments, he will always be remembered in connection with his Grand Canyon descent as one of America's greatest explorers.

Before Powell's boats reached the Grand Canyon proper, when he was still in Glen Canyon, he first discovered that earlier people had lived in this rugged country. He identified "ruins" and recorded that they were built by ancestors of the Hopi Indians, who he knew resided in the large pueblo villages to the south. He speculated that the former inhabitants had built stone houses in these isolated locations because "centuries ago . . . nomadic tribes were sweeping down upon them and they resorted to these cliffs and canyons for safety."

On August 11, 1869, soon after entering the Grand Canyon, at the mouth of the Little Colorado River, Powell made his first archaeological discovery within the canyon itself. He had climbed the cliff above the river to determine his latitude and longitude and to measure the height of the walls, while his crew carried out the routine activities necessitated by the rigors of river travel, drying out the food and repairing the boats. As he walked down the gorge at the foot of the cliff, he "discovered a trail, deeply worn in the rock . . . in some places, steps have been cut. I can see no evidence of its having been traveled for a long time. It was doubtless a path used by the people who inhabited this country anterior to the present Indian races. . . . I returned to camp . . . and find that some of the men have discovered ruins, and many fragments of pottery; also, etching and hieroglyphs on the rocks."

A few days later Powell and his men stopped at a lively, clear-flowing creek, a striking contrast to the muddy waters he had seen upstream at a place he had called Dirty Devil. He named this watercourse Bright Angel Creek and noted the ruins of "two or three old houses, which were originally of stone, laid in mortar. . . . In one room I find an old mealing stone, deeply worn, as if it had been much used. A great deal of pottery is strewn around, and old trails." Again speculating that the people who left these remains must have been farmers like the Hopis, this time Powell surmised that they had come to the canyon to escape the Spaniards: "These old Spanish conquerors had a monstrous greed for gold, and a wonderful lust for saving souls. Treasure they must have, if not on earth, why, then in heaven; and when they failed to find heathen temples, decked with silver, they propitiated Heaven by seizing the heathen themselves."

Later in the expedition, Powell discovered other remains of ancient peoples, as well as those of the Paiute Indians, who farmed along the bank of the river. By the time his great adventure was over, he had

John Wesley Powell and a Paiute Indian. Photo by John K. Hillers, Powell Expedition. Courtesy Smithsonian Institution.

also completed the first chapter of archaeological research in the Grand Canyon. Yet, as always, there were many more questions than answers. While he had found the remains of some old Indian settlements, he was not sure who had made them, when they were made, why the people had decided to live within the rugged canyon, what their life there was like, and why they had left.

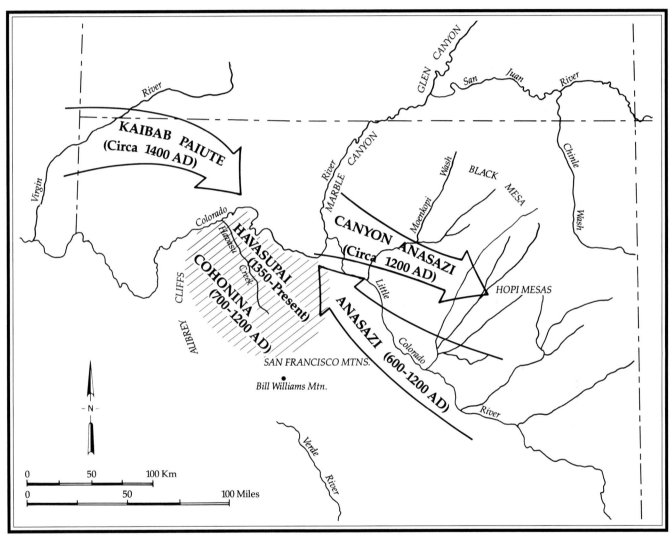

Assumed movements of post-Archaic cultures in the Grand Canyon.
Drawing by Katrina Lasko.

An Outline of Grand Canyon Prehistory

Over a hundred years of archaeological research in the Grand Canyon, much of it concentrated in the last fifty years, have followed Powell's first investigations. Many of the questions that may have crossed his mind now have preliminary answers, but a far more complex story of the canyon's human past has emerged than he would have imagined.

The earliest evidence of the canyon's human use can be seen in remains found in secret ritual caves and spectacular drawings on rock walls produced several thousand years ago by hunters and gatherers of the Early Archaic period. Centuries later, about A.D. 700, the first settled existence began when the people of the Cohonina culture moved to the territory south of the canyon, the same area that was to be occupied in historic time by the Havasupais. The Cohonina may have arrived from the west. At about the same time, another farming people, the Anasazi, came into the canyon region from the east; eventually, they were to become its most numerous and prominent settlers.

For a time, in the A.D. 1000s and 1100s, the Anasazi occupied hundreds of sites on the South Rim and deep within the canyon. They even pushed the limits of their agricultural technology to farm high on the cool Kaibab Plateau north of the canyon. The archaeological record reveals the struggles of the Anasazi and Cohonina and their desperate attempts to live in the region's rugged environment.

At a time of severe drought near the end of the 1100s, both groups left the area. But while the Cohonina were not to be heard from again, the time the Anasazi had spent in the canyon was not to be forgotten. For today the Hopis continue to tell how their ancestors emerged from an opening in the depths of the canyon and, until recently, groups of Hopi men returned there to commemorate the beginnings of their people.

The Havasupais, who arrived in the 1300s, occupied the canyons and plateau in the southwest part of what is today the national park. During the same late prehistoric period, another tribe, the hunting and gathering Paiutes, also moved onto the plateau and into the canyons north of the Colorado River. With their appearance, the prehistory of the Grand Canyon seems to have come full circle, for their life must have been similar in many ways to that of the region's first inhabitants—the foraging magicians of Archaic time.

The overall picture that has emerged from the study of Grand Canyon prehistory is one of a succession of peoples who moved into the region and for a time adjusted to its harsh environment and meager resources. In various ways they scratched out a living on the margins of the more productive lands and developed cultures to the east and south. But eventually, in response to changes in climate and perhaps for other reasons we do not yet fully understand, most of these people moved away or succumbed to the rigors of the Grand Canyon region — one of nature's most beautiful and yet most demanding environments.

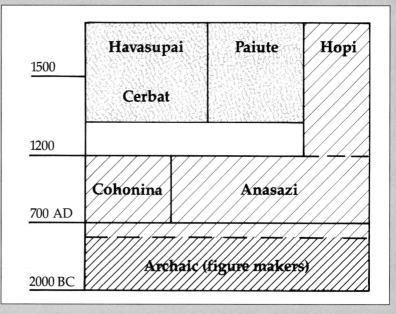

General relationship of Grand Canyon cultures.

The Grand Canyon. Illustration for John Wesley Powell's *Report on the Exploration of the Colorado River.*

Chapter III

Pictographs from the Shaman's Gallery. Drawing by Polly Schaafsma.

Seeking the Canyon Magicians

Split-willow twig figurines found in caves in the Grand Canyon. Photo by David Noble.

Having picked our way up the rocks for nearly an hour, we came to the cave opening in the Redwall formation. From here I could look both into the cave mouth and out over the magnificent Grand Canyon. Let's stop for a breather before we go in," I called to my companion, Art Lange.

My pack was getting heavier than I cared to say, and I sank down on the nearest rock. The year before, I had been sitting by a campfire on the South Rim when Art and Raymond deSaussure came up and introduced themselves. They had been conducting a survey of caves. "So far Ray and I have been in 150 caves in the canyon. In four, something very curious has shown up that perhaps you can explain to us."

They described small fragments of twisted and tied willow branches, obviously man-made, and one little figurine of this material. It sounded like nothing I was familiar with, and I was not prepared for the object they showed me. It was by far the most appealing artifact I had ever seen, not quite the size of my hand, in the form of a deer-like animal. It had a definite ageless charm.

Because I hoped to learn as much as possible about the prehistory of the canyon, I didn't hesitate to say, "Let's put together a small expedition and see what we can learn about this."

We raised a small sum of money for supplies, and a year later, on a moonlit August night in 1955, each with a fifty-pound pack of food and equipment, we descended the Kaibab Trail. By midmorning we reached a side canyon called Cremation, and the sun was beaming down. "I know exactly how this place was named," Ray remarked.

When we reached the cave, Art asked how I planned to go about investigating it. Beyond an entrance littered with huge boulders, a dusty, fairly flat floor receded into the darkness.

"We should excavate some test pits in stratigraphic levels in the cave floor near the entrance," I said authoritatively. "That's where the people probably lived and where most of their trash should be. From these remains we can reconstruct the whole story and fit the figurines into their way of life."

All this was announced with the complete confidence possessed only by a new Ph.D. in archaeology. I had just completed my dissertation on the prehistory of the Havasupai Indians. In 1955 almost no archaeological work had been carried out in the Grand Canyon itself. What little we knew suggested that Indian farmers had settled the rim areas in the A.D. 700s and gradually worked their way into the canyon proper; but all this was still a rather hazy outline. I had no idea that our cave expedition would give a completely new dimension to this story.

Next morning we began digging. In semidarkness, we measured out test pits in precise three-meter squares, then dug down in ten-centimeter levels so we could plot the location of everything we found. Carefully, I examined each shovelful, knowing the answers must lie just below. I told Art and Ray that once we reached any evidence that people had lived there — for example, the remains of an old campfire — we would use trowels and camel's-hair brushes. However, it did not turn out at all the way I had planned. After three days, I finally admitted to myself that I was completely wrong. Absolutely nothing had shown up in the excavations.

To hide my embarrassment, I said, "Well, at least we know for sure they didn't live in the cave. The question now is, did you two find the only figurine? And if so, how did it get here?"

As we disconsolately packed up to leave, I wandered around the edges of the cave, flashlight in hand. I had barely looked in the direction of the cave walls because of the tunnel vision created by my certainty of how to proceed. Now, in a pack rat's nest, I spotted fragments of twisted willow — and then my eyes focused on a pile of rock two feet high. It looked suspiciously unnatural, like a small cairn piled on a mountaintop by climbers.

I shouted for Art and Ray. They came rushing over, and cautiously, we peeled back the rocks. At the bottom of the pile strands of twisted willow appeared through the dust. First one figurine was uncovered, then others. Each one was dusted off with a paintbrush, photographed, and recorded. When we finished, we counted thirty-two complete figurines in one small, scooped-out basin.

As we removed each one, we noted its depth, orientation, and placement in relationship to the others, for at this point we had no idea what might be important, and we certainly did not want to miss anything. Shredded juniper bark and clumps of grass had been placed between layers of figurines. Each figurine was about the size of a small hand and made of a single twig of willow. Some had what appeared to be horns and some a wrapping of grass around the body, but all were obviously made to a common pattern.

I had several obvious clues to the significance of the figurines. They had been found in caves not used for living purposes, and extremely difficult to reach. Their placement under the rock cairn suggested a special importance. Moreover, several had been pierced with small sticks — undoubtedly, miniature spears. I began to realize I was working in what had been a ritual cave.

The exhilaration that followed this breakthrough was one I will never forget. There is something almost mystical in realizing you have stepped back in time and seen in some detail the life of another people. And therein lies the reward and frustration of archaeology: to visit the past, only to be trapped by a fog that just occasionally rises enough to allow a partial and tantalizing view of what had happened there. I knew I would probably learn very little more about these figurine makers.

During one of our long, hot, inner-canyon evenings, Ray summed up the matter: "How ironic. We seem to have discovered so much about one small part of what must have been secret ritual, while much of their everyday life will probably always remain at the level of speculation." Regretfully, I agreed.

Almost a quarter of a century has passed. More figurines have been found in the caves of the region. Much has been learned about its ecology. But Ray's prediction has held true.

Yet I have always felt fortunate that this, one of my earliest professional projects, contained so many elements that make the study of the past such a fascinating field. The adventure and excitement of the unknown. The systematic work leading to the accumulation of small clues. The conclusions drawn, some based on the immediate data and some from secondary inferences. And then a reconstruction of part of the past.

Looking back, I do not regret dealing with a hunting band while some of my friends were beginning work on temple mounds in the Mississippi Valley or great Maya cities. Later, I was to direct complex projects that took years to excavate and a decade to unravel, but here, in one season, I had the opportunity to see a project through and gain rare insight into a way of life similar to that of my own remote ancestors and those of the American Indians.

A figurine cave in the Grand Canyon. Photo by Karl Kernberger, 1970. School of American Research.

Early Archaic Hunters and Magic Ritual

The first human occupants of the New World, called Paleo-Indians by archaeologists, arrived near the end of the Ice Age. They lived by ranging widely over the land, hunting large Pleistocene mammals like the bison and mammoth, and foraging for a variety of smaller game and wild plants. As the Ice Age drew to a close and the climate became warmer and dryer, the big game gradually died off, hastened by the skill of the early hunters.

In the newly developing environment, about 5000 B.C., the early American Indians began to hunt more small game and gather an even wider range of wild plants. In time the population of what we now call Archaic people grew. Each group, having less land available, was forced to adapt to life in a smaller territory with its own combination of resources. Out of this limitation of land grew a number of more regionally specialized, though roughly similar foraging ways of life, each with its own particular cultural stamp.

Archaic use of the Grand Canyon area began about 2000 B.C. Unlike the usual remains of hunting and gathering peoples — generally only the bare leavings of camp life — the evidence from the Grand Canyon Archaic is not at all mundane. Although magic was widely practiced throughout the world, clear evidence of it is seldom recovered in the debris of prehistoric sites. Yet deep in the canyon, Archaic people left a dramatic record of magic ritual and images they felt were important to understanding the world around them, both providing an intriguing glimpse into the early prehistory of the American Southwest.

The story of Archaic magic in the Grand Canyon has now been discovered in ten caves, each containing caches of small animal figurines; seven other caves have been found from southern California to southern Utah. The figurines were all made following one pattern. Each was constructed from split willow branches, cottonwood, or occasionally other materials, then deposited in shallow depressions in the sand of a cave floor and covered with rock cairns. Each cache contained up to dozens of figurines about the size of an open hand or smaller, and some of the figurines were pierced with small spears. In many of the figurine caves, remains of extinct mountain goats and bighorn sheep have been found, and some figurines contained the pelleted droppings of these animals in their body cavities.

Many of the caves in the canyon were isolated and nearly inaccessible, high above the canyon floor in the limestone Redwall cliffs. But other than the figurines themselves, the caves contained essentially no evidence that people had been there. Radiocarbon dating has placed the manufacture of the figurines between 2000 and 1000 B.C.

Down the centuries and throughout the world, people have believed that they can control supernatural powers by following

Desert bighorn sheep. Photo by John Running.

Pictograph panel, Shaman's Gallery, Grand Canyon. Photo by Polly Schaafsma.

magical rituals, on the assumption that the actions of the world are tied together by powerful supernatural forces that can be controlled if the correct procedures are known and performed with exactitude. Anthropologists have called one of these methods imitative magic. In his great work *The Golden Bough*, Sir James Frazer described a classic example: "When . . . an Ojibway Indian desires to work evil on any one, he makes a little wooden image of his enemy and runs a needle into its head or heart, or shoots an arrow into it, believing that wherever the needle pierces or the arrow strikes the image, his foe will at the same instant be seized with a sharp pain." We are all familiar with the process from those grade B voodoo movies we saw as kids.

All the elements of imitative magic were apparent in the figurine caves of the Grand Canyon, and as a result, we can construct a picture of what may have occurred at the time they were deposited in the caves. The facts surrounding their discovery, combined with what is known about the lives of other hunting and gathering people, observations on magic ritual performed by shamans, and a bit of literary license enable us to weave together a story of the kind of events that may have occurred in this long-vanished culture.

About 2000 B.C., many seminomadic Western Archaic bands lived throughout the region around the Grand Canyon. These small groups of relatives moved with the changing seasons through their territory, taking advantage of whatever was available for food. In spring and summer, women collected buds, fruits, and seeds in the varied environments of the canyon and on the plateaus, and men hunted small animals throughout the year. In the fall, deer could be found in larger

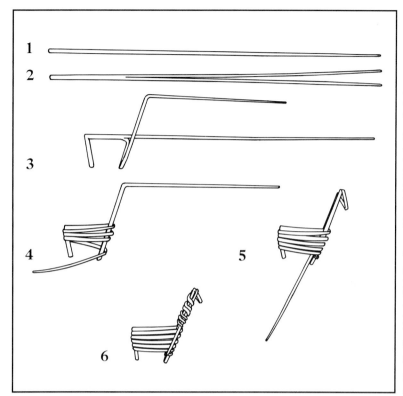

Construction of a split-twig figurine.
Drawing by Katrina Lasko.

than normal numbers in the forests of the plateau, and piñon nuts were especially abundant.

The foraging bands made simple shelters — windbreaks of brush covering a few logs lined up against one another — so when they left one of their temporary seasonal camps, little would remain behind, perhaps only the pine boughs they had gathered for sleeping nests. Valuables like rabbit-fur blankets and stone knives would be left only if they were damaged beyond repair.

Each winter men from the band converged on a few selected side canyons with just the right combination of water and restricted access — the best places to hunt the protein-rich desert bighorn sheep. The sheep need water every day, and when they were drinking they were most vulnerable to experienced hunters. But, even in the best of circumstances, the bighorns were extremely difficult to kill, so the hunters prepared carefully for their coming challenge, reinforcing their luck and skill with a traditional magic ritual to help ensure the success of the coming hunt.

The hunters descended into the canyon on an old, well-marked animal trail. Hiking to a certain side canyon, one of the few that contained water, they gathered a number of willow branches, carefully selecting only those of the correct thickness, length, and flexibility. With these in hand, they climbed up the dry bed of the side canyon toward the base of the great red-walled limestone cliff that held their sacred cave. Scrambling to the top of the rock talus at the base of the cliff, they picked their way from rock to rock up to the mouth of the cave. The older men had made this journey many times, but it would have been the first for the younger hunters, who must have been a little apprehensive about learning the secrets of the ancients.

Once inside the cave, the group would silently watch the one among them who was a hunting shaman, for he knew the exact ritual to perform. First he constructed the figurines, splitting a willow branch for most of its length and then bending the unsplit end to make the rear leg and back. The other split section was bent to make the front leg, neck, head, nose, and, in some cases, horns. Finally, the remaining part of the first split section was wrapped around the legs to make the body.

When the necessary number of figurines had been produced (we do not know if one or more were made at each visit), the shaman may have worked further magic to tie the ritual even more closely to the hunted animal, implanting some with a pellet of bighorn dung or piercing them with small spears to replicate what was to occur in the coming hunt. The killing of a bighorn sheep was also visualized, and powerful chants and incantations were recited, some so old that their meaning had been lost. All of these actions were firmly based on the belief that chance does not exist; rather, through the power of ritual, it is the mind that controls events.

A shallow basin was then scooped out of the dust floor near the side wall of the cave, and the figurines were reverently laid into place and covered with shredded juniper bark or bundles of grass. Finally, the hole was covered with fairly large rocks to mark the cache.

The hunters then left the cave and traveled into the canyon to stalk the bighorn sheep, secure in the knowledge that they had done all that was possible to ensure their hunting success. Only a mistake made in the ritual could cause them to fail.

While it is not known exactly how long the magical effigies were made, sometime between 1500 and 1000 B.C. their use was discontinued. But we do have one other possible insight into the culture of these Archaic figurine makers, and just as rare a view as that provided by the figurines themselves. Only recently, in the western part of Grand Canyon National Park, a wondrous series of prehistoric paintings were discovered on a natural rock wall called the "Shaman's Gallery." These pictographs have been described by Polly Schaafsma, an expert on southwestern rock art, whose earlier classic work on the subject was published in the School of American Research Southwest Indian Art series. Schaafsma has described the drawings as "over 40 bizarre, elongated anthropomorphic figures" along with intricate designs and figures representing bighorn sheep, deer, carnivores, and snakes. On the basis of their style, she dates them sometime between 2000 B.C. and A.D. 1, so while it is impossible to tell for sure if they were painted by the same people who made the figurines, they are well within the same Archaic time range.

The meaning behind these drawings, like that of the figurines, will never be known for sure, but they clearly seem to have been part of an important ritual. I would stress once again how strange it is that we should know so little about the everyday life of these Archaic people and yet have such a dramatic glimpse into the secret aspects of their spiritual life. However, we can obtain important insights into the life of the most ancient canyon dwellers by relating their way of life to that of the later foraging Paiutes.

Pictograph from the Shaman's Gallery. From a drawing by Polly Schaafsma.

Prehistoric Cultures and Living Peoples

Archaeologists can recover many concrete details about past cultures, but some aspects of life leave no material remains and are lost to us, such as religious feelings, personal intentions, music, and social relationships. For this reason, archaeologists often study the culture of living peoples to gain a broader view of what a past culture may have been like. While no two ways of life are ever exactly the same, the greater the number of similarities between a prehistoric and living culture, the more insights can be gained.

Archaic culture, for example, can reasonably be compared to that of the Kaibab Paiutes. Both lived around the North Rim, and both led a foraging existence. Yet even with these similarities, knowledge of a historic culture may not expose all the details of a prehistoric one. Archaic peoples lived thousands of years before the Paiutes and used spears for hunting, for example, while Paiutes also had the more efficient bow and arrow. But the detailed information available about living peoples can certainly serve as an effective guide for thinking about how life was lived in the past.

We are fortunate in the study of Grand Canyon archaeology that each of the prehistoric cultures can be coupled with and compared to a historic one living in the same area whose non-material culture has been studied in some detail. Just as Archaic peoples are comparable to the Kaibab Paiutes, so the Cohonina culture can be compared to the traditional lifestyle of the canyon's living residents, the Havasupais. Similarly, a study of the culture and religion of the Hopis puts us in a better position to say what Anasazi life may have been like. Such comparisons have added great richness to our understanding of the prehistoric cultures of the Grand Canyon.

Prehistoric	Historic
ARCHAIC -----------	PAIUTE
COHONINA -----------	HAVASUPAI
ANASAZI -----------	HOPI

Similar prehistoric-historic Grand Canyon cultures.

Artist's rendering of Anasazi climbing out of the canyon. Drawing by Robert W. Nicholson.

Chapter IV

Paiute family on the Kaibab Plateau. Photo by John K. Hillers, Powell Expedition, 1871–75.
Courtesy Smithsonian Institution.

The Canyon's Last Hunters and Gatherers: The Kaibab Paiutes

Following the Archaic period, two new cultures, the Cohonina and the Anasazi, appeared in the Grand Canyon region. Farming allowed them to lead more settled lives than those who practiced an Archaic way of life. They built more substantial habitations, made pottery, and most important for the archaeologist, left more remains. Their story, central to Grand Canyon archaeology, will be told in subsequent sections.

Eventually, these farming peoples also left the canyon and its environs. North of the Colorado River, their place was later taken by the Kaibab Paiutes. The Paiutes entered the Grand Canyon region during the prehistoric period, but they were still living in their aboriginal territory and in some respects leading their traditional way of life when John Wesley Powell and other anthropologists visited and described them in some detail. Their culture was similar enough to that of the Archaic people that I have chosen to describe the Kaibab Paiutes next in order to provide a model of a foraging culture.

After the Anasazi left the Grand Canyon area, the plateau and canyon north of the Colorado River remained unoccupied for perhaps two centuries. While little archaeological evidence has been found relating to the Kaibab Paiutes, some relatively clear conclusions about the prehistoric movements of their ancestors can be made from linguistic analysis. By A.D. 1400 they had spread into the region as part of a movement of Uto-Aztecan-speaking people who had begun pushing east from the foothills of the Sierra Nevadas in southeastern California about A.D. 1000.

Historically, the territory of the Kaibab Paiutes ranged from the Grand Canyon on the south, Kanab Creek on the west, Para Creek on the east, and the northeastern drainages of the Virgin River on the north. Their range spanned many environments, from the bottom of the hot, dry desert of the inner canyon to the high plateaus of the north. There, spruce and fir forest over 9,000 feet in elevation, interspersed with mountain meadows, dropped down through stands of pine to more open areas of juniper, piñon, sage, and eventually, mesquite. For a hunting and gathering people, this territory provided a valuable diversity of food and materials.

The Kaibab Paiutes, like most foragers, moved through their territory in a relatively fixed yearly schedule, taking advantage of the foods that were most readily available in any one season. They would travel in bands and stay in a particular camp long enough to harvest the plants and animals within walking distance before moving to the next location.

Bands varied greatly in number, typically consisting of a small group of related brothers, their wives, and small children — usually three households of some ten individuals each. Each household was composed of a nuclear family of parents and their unmarried children, a few grandparents, and some unattached relatives like aunts. Political control was mostly advisory. A "chief" or headman, when anyone held such authority, was usually an older man in the group. He would be "good," "generous," "smart," "energetic," and "able to talk well."

The annual cycle of Kaibab Paiute life illustrates the different ways they adapted to their varied environment. Summer was a good time of the year. Many bands camped by traditionally owned springs, and a variety of food was available. Clothing was simple during the warm months. Older men went naked, and others usually wore an apron of skin or vegetable fiber, perhaps a skin or basketry cap, and bark or yucca sandals or no footwear at all.

Shelters were also simple, mainly un-walled shades made of upright poles roofed with matted branches or dome-shaped huts made by arranging poles in a circle, bent over and intertwined with twigs. Men moved out from the camps, using bows and arrows or traps to hunt the available game: deer, mountain sheep, antelope, squirrels, marmots, chipmunks, wood rats, porcupines, and badgers. Women and children stayed closer to the camp, collecting seeds, fruits, and berries and taking them back to the camp in conical burden baskets suspended by a tumpline across the forehead.

Kaibab Paiutes. Powell Expedition, 1871–75. Courtesy Grand Canyon National Park, National Park Service.

Mouth-open was the head man of one band, and something of his life is known in detail from the research of Isabel Kelly, an anthropologist from the University of California who studied the Paiutes in the 1940s. By following his movements it is possible to gain the kind of insight into the activities of a people, the real flesh of their life, that is never possible to recover from purely archaeological research.

Mouth-open traditionally used Cane Spring, at the base of the Kaibab Plateau. He lived there during the spring and summer, close to other camps in the area. In the fall the band moved on to the Kaibab Plateau, where several other bands from throughout the region converged. The groups were well known to Mouth-open because they had been traveling together for most of the previous year.

The fall was also a time of plenty. Not only were the yucca fruits ripening, but in many years the highly nutritious piñon nuts could be collected, and deer were always plentiful on the plateau. With the cooler temperatures on the plateau, many of the men now wore poncho-like buckskin shirts, and a few carried rabbitskin blankets.

Traveling to a new location, the women carried some household goods in their burden baskets, such as a horn spoon, a wooden bowl, and a pitch-covered water jug. The men, in addition to a bow and some arrows, took a leather pouch with a few gaming items, some firemaking equipment, and a tool to process hides. The group could get most of what else they needed from the forest.

When Mouth-open and his group moved to the plateau, they usually met the shaman Alkali Man, whose band lived in six camps — his own and those of his five married sons. They usually joined Bull Lizard and his two married brothers, the three camps of To Get Well, and Dog Eye, from Cave Water Spring. When the people from these camps and nearly five hundred other people from elsewhere in the Kaibab Paiute territory moved to the plateau, they had a chance to visit friends and relatives whom they saw only at this time of year. It was also the best opportunity for young people to be on the lookout for a potential mate.

Camps were set up in the dense fir and spruce forest, preferably close to a spring, far enough from the meadows not to disturb the game, but close enough for stalking. Camp locations were known from previous years; gentle hillsides were favored because the slope promoted runoff in case of rain. The remains of previous encampments could be seen under nearby trees, but Mouth-open and the others never camped in exactly the same place twice, knowing that trash from an earlier use could draw flies.

The shelters at the camp were made simply because they would be needed for only one season. Pine boughs collected from nearby were set against one another to form a circular enclosure under the overhanging branches of a low tree. The boughs cut the wind but still allowed the warmth of the sun to penetrate the shelter. A fire was built below the covering to provide warmth, increasingly important through the fall because of the cool temperatures at the high altitude of the plateau. In a very bad storm people sought shelter under a rock overhang, but they were known to be unhealthy and the home of bad spirits, so they were avoided whenever possible.

Kaibab Paiute summer house. Photo by K. Hillers, Powell Expedition, 1871–75. Courtesy Smithsonian Institution.

Every morning after the camps had gathered on the plateau, the headman chosen from those assembled spoke to the group, telling them where and how they could approach the hunt. Their strategy might involve circling the deer and driving them toward the headman. Kaibab Paiutes hunted with arrows made of serviceberry branches and tipped with stone points held on by sinew. Eagle feathers attached to the end of the shaft helped guide the arrows.

If they were fortunate in the hunt, the meat would be shared throughout the group. Although the man who led the groups during the fall was not a chief during the rest of the year, everyone respected

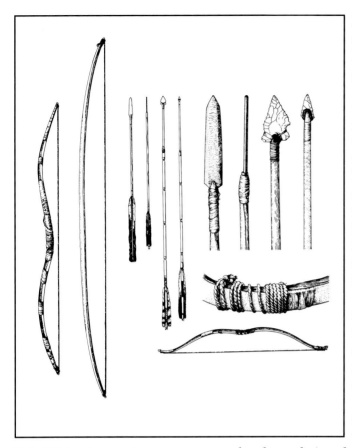

Kaibab Paiute bows and arrows.

him, realizing it was important to have a leader and cooperate in the hunting season. Out of respect for his services, each hunter would also make sure he gave the chief part of his kill.

As winter approached and snow accumulated, the people broke up again into small bands and moved to lower and warmer quarters. Some of them went to the rim of the Grand Canyon, while others traveled east to Houserock Valley or Antelope Valley. During the winter, living could be extremely difficult. Mescal leaves were roasted, leftover berries were gathered, and rabbits, whose tracks could be followed in the snow, were killed. The men, hunting in snowshoes, also drove rabbits into nets, where they were trapped and clubbed. But the snow made it quite difficult to hunt larger animals.

In the cold months small family groups lived in the mouths of caves or rock overhangs, which they blocked with juniper branches for added comfort. They also stuffed their yucca sandals with rabbit fur and wore rabbitskin blankets to help ward off the cold.

During the long winter evenings stories were told, which once begun had to be finished — otherwise, winter might run into summer. The tales might be about their culture hero and trickster, Coyote, how he stole fire for the benefit of mankind, established menstrual and birth customs, and instructed mankind how to tie bowstrings; or how, after the animals were originally made of mud, Coyote gave them their names.

Food was scarce well into early spring, and the people depended heavily on stored food such as dried mescal leaves, juniper berries, and cactus blooms. Pemmican had also been stored earlier, made by mixing lean dried meat with melted fat to form a paste that was pressed into cakes and flavored with currants or other berries for taste. Stored food was of critical importance to the Kaibab Paiutes, as it was to all the foragers in the basin and plateau area. They spent a great deal of effort over all of the rest of the year gathering and storing food for the winter. They had experienced enough grim winters of near starvation in the past, and thinking ahead became of utmost importance to their survival.

As the snows thawed with the approach of spring, foraging again became easier. Eggs of quail and grouse could be gathered, and migratory ducks were hunted in the ponds that dotted the plateau. Locusts and caterpillar grubs were collected and parched, or roasted or dried between hot stones. Hunting could also begin again, and grasses, berries, and chokecherries could now be gathered. Then, as spring moved into summer, the annual cycle began again, as it had for hundreds of years.

Whenever a death occurred among the Kaibab Paiutes, relatives prepared the corpse for burial. The dead person's property was destroyed, including any eagles they had owned. Those involved in the burial then bathed and abstained from meat, salt, and intercourse for four days. The family or the entire camp then moved away from the place where the death had occurred, at least for a time. During a period of mourning, women cut their hair. The name of the dead person was never spoken again.

In 1776, Spanish priests including Silvestre Vélez de Escalante, the first Europeans to encounter the Kaibab Paiutes, found them living essentially aboriginal lives. By the early 1800s the Paiutes were being baptized in Spanish settlements in the upper Rio Grande and in southern California, and the Spaniards were taking Indian slaves. Isabel Kelly and Catherine Fowler, in an excellent article on the Southern Paiutes in the *Handbook of North American Indians*, quote the trader Farnham as reporting that, in 1839, Paiutes were "hunted in the spring of the year, when weak and helpless . . . and when taken, [they were] fattened, carried to Santa Fe and sold as slaves during their minority."

By the middle of the 1800s, many Paiutes had already been driven out of the more favorable areas of their old territory, and those that remained had to compete for their land with the Mormon settlers who were moving into the region. In 1873, a federal commission headed by John Wesley Powell recommended moving the remaining Paiutes to reservations. Their problems with the newcomers continued for the next quarter of a century, and not until the beginning of the twentieth century did their population begin to achieve some modicum of successful life in the new world of foreigners.

We know less about the Kaibab Paiutes than we do about many other foragers around the world, for example, the African Bushmen, the Australian aborigines, or the Eskimos. These cultures were still functioning in their traditional forms when anthropologists began studying them, but the Kaibab Paiutes had already been so greatly changed by the impact of Western civilization that their original culture could be reconstructed only from memory. Yet every time I have walked the great forests north of the Grand Canyon, knowing this is where the Kaibab Paiutes lived, I am thankful that we know as many details of their life as we do, giving us just that much better an idea of the life led by their Archaic predecessors.

Chapter V

Piñon forest, Coconino Plateau. Photo by Douglas W. Schwartz. School of American Research.

First Encounter at Red Butte

On the vast, forested plateau south of the Grand Canyon, the air was filled with the exhilarating smell of piñon trees. In this arid country, there were no surface streams to be seen, only a few kinds of trees, and none of the rolling landscape I was used to. It was another world for me, completely different from the well-watered, humid, botanically varied woodlands of the East I had grown up in. But the strangeness of the landscape only added to the excitement of setting out on a new archaeological adventure.

I was twenty and had finished my junior year at the University of Kentucky, majoring in anthropology. Working from there, and beginning while I was still in high school, I had already taken part in three archaeological field projects, perhaps one of the reasons I had been chosen as one of ten students from throughout the United States and Canada by John McGregor of the University of Illinois to join his 1949 field project in northern Arizona.

The project was an important effort to investigate the enigmatic Cohonina culture in what was thought to be their heartland, south of the Grand Canyon. When I applied for a place on the crew, the chance for a wilderness adventure was uppermost in my mind. But a summer in the West also offered all the elements that made the study of archaeology so satisfying: the thrill of possible discovery; the chance to learn more about field work; being part of an effort that was involved in the search for ideas; and the opportunity to be in the company of others with similar tastes, people who had experienced their own archaeological adventures and who would be willing to share what they had learned. So as we drove west from Urbana to Flagstaff, then north toward the canyon, I could hardly contain my joy.

When we arrived at our camp near Red Butte, deep within the forest, the tents had already been set up by an old friend of Dr. McGregor, Milton Wetherall. Milt was a member of the famous Mesa Verde Wetherall family, who had been so active in the early days of discovering southwestern prehistory. At the time I did not realize how my association with Milt was tying me into the early history of southwestern archaeology. He was the first real cowboy I had met. I will never forget the tremendous power in his weatherbeaten hands, which he did not fail to demonstrate to an eastern greenhorn like me. I soon learned to avoid shaking hands with him, but over the next decade he and I became good friends.

Seventeen sites were excavated that summer, and each student was responsible for work on one or more of them. An added bonus were the Hopi and Havasupai laborers who had been hired to help with the digging. It was always enjoyable to know and work with them, and I continued an association with one of the Havasupais, Charlie Wescogomie, until his suicide in the 1960s. After the field portion of the project was completed, the crew moved to the Museum of Northern Arizona in Flagstaff, the cosponsoring institution. Here we completed the laboratory work, and each crew member took responsibility for writing up the results of some phase of the project.

My work in Kentucky had been on prominent burial mounds and large, late prehistoric villages. In contrast, the Cohonina sites seemed small, scattered throughout the seemingly trackless forest, and isolated from one another. So I was left with the impression that there had never been many Cohonina and that their way of life had been simple and extremely difficult. At the time, none of us could have known just how hard it would be for us and others over the next forty years to fathom the true nature of Cohonina culture, but in 1949, I was far from such concerns. I was just happy to be doing archaeology.

The Cohonina:
Origin and Fate Unknown

About the beginning of the A.D. 700s, the Cohonina appeared south of the Grand Canyon, apparently with a way of life in transition between foraging and farming. For several centuries they covered a territory of nearly 3,600 square miles centered on the Coconino Plateau and extending south to about the Bill Williams and San Francisco mountains; west beyond Havasu Canyon to the Aubrey Cliffs; and east, beyond the edge of the Coconino Plateau, to the drainage of the Little Colorado River.

Cohonina culture was first recognized by Lyndon Hargrave of the Museum of Northern Arizona. He borrowed the name from a Hopi word meaning "people who live to the west," but the Hopis were probably using the word to refer to a group who entered this territory somewhat later, the Havasupais. The Cohonina culture was separated from the others around it on the basis of a pottery type, San Francisco Mountain Gray ware, along with other distinguishing traits of stone-work and architecture.

The territory of the Cohonina ranged in elevation from 2,500 feet in the canyon to between 4,000 and 9,000 feet on the plateau. The country looks today as it probably did when they occupied it: a desert-like canyon cut by ribbons of green where there is water, and on the plateau, partially forested piñon-juniper woodland with stands of ponderosa pine growing in the higher elevations, on mountain slopes, and near the edge of the Grand Canyon. Within the wooded areas and at lower elevations are interspersed parcels of open grassland.

Water has always been scarce in this environment. There are very few surface streams and only scattered springs. The average yearly precipitation is about sixteen inches, much of it falling as snow in winter or as rain in late summer. Nevertheless, it is a land of abundant game, including mule deer, antelope, cottontail rabbits, jackrabbits, squirrels, raccoons, mountain lions, bobcats, badgers, coyotes, bears, and desert bighorn sheep.

It is generally agreed when the Cohonina came to the Grand Canyon region, but there is no clear consensus on where they came from. Some feel they developed in place, growing out of the resident Archaic population of foragers, adding agriculture and pottery, and thus being recognized by archaeologists as a separate culture. Others believe there is no strong evidence for this kind of evolutionary process, rather, that the Cohonina arrived from the west, as suggested from the way they manufactured their pottery.

But there is no reason to believe that the Cohonina way of life developed from a single direct source: commonly, cultures take on an amalgam of traits from many adjacent neighbors. Perhaps the ancestors of the Cohonina were a resident Archaic population living south of the Grand Canyon who learned some agriculture from the Anasazi to the east. With a somewhat more settled life, they then could have learned the paddle-and-anvil technique of making pottery (in which the clay coils are paddled flat) from the people to the west and their styles of pottery design and firing methods from the Anasazi. Whatever the origins of the Cohonina, it is certainly possible, as with so many other cultures, that they were a mixed breed.

If it is not clear where the Cohonina came from, it is equally unclear how they made their living. While it is assumed that hunting and gathering were important to them, only small numbers of animal bones have been found in their sites: rabbits, rats, squirrels, prairie dogs, antelope, deer, and birds.

The more vital question is how much farming they practiced. Neighbors on both the south and east were practicing farming, so they would have been familiar with horticulture. But some archaeologists feel that the Cohonina did not farm at all, judging from the virtual absence of domesticated plant remains at excavated sites. Only a few charred corn kernels, cob fragments, corn pollen grains, and squash seeds have been found, all of which, it is argued, could have been obtained in trade.

Alan Sullivan, an archaeologist with the University of Cincinnati, has proposed a reconstruction of their economic life in Prehistory of the Upper Basin, Coconino County, Arizona, based on analogies with contemporary foraging peoples:

> The Cohonina most likely never occupied a particular settlement on a year-round basis. . . . When . . . base camps were established it most likely involved moving the entire household from the main settlement. At the base camps, members of Cohonina households ranged out into the environment on a multiple-day basis, . . . not necessarily return[ing] to camp each evening. . . . [H]unting parties composed exclusively of males often stayed away from the main encampment for several days at a time, while foraging parties consisting of females and adolescents stayed close to and returned to the encampment daily.

Sullivan is describing a way of life similar to that of Archaic peoples, and later, the Paiutes.

Those who favor the position that the Cohonina were farmers, as I do, argue not only from the few plant remains, but also from a complex of other traits usually associated with a more settled way of life: terracing, substantial architecture, and pottery. While none of these traits alone is enough to support the argument, their combination makes it reasonable.

Associated with several Cohonina sites are what appear to be rock check dams, which may have been used to hold back rainwater for irrigating crops. But it is the larger architectural features that appear to go far beyond what foragers had the time or need to build. Although the Cohonina did build temporary brush structures of the kind used by foragers, they also built more substantial structures that changed in

Cohonina pottery. Drawing by Katrina Lasko.

design and size over time. Their early habitations were pithouses, which were partially dug into the ground, but later they built above-ground masonry room blocks and thick-walled structures with large rooms, doors, roofs, and other features requiring an ample investment of time. Also, such constructions imply more of a commitment to one place than would be usual for a foraging people in a marginal environment.

The Cohonina also made significant amounts of pottery. While it was not as technically or aesthetically fine as that of their Anasazi neighbors, it clearly served their purposes well enough to continue as a ceramic tradition for centuries. Ceramics are made by nonagricultural people, but rarely in the quantity, variety of forms, or with the elaborate decoration of Cohonina pottery.

In assessing these alternatives, it must be considered that Cohonina studies are still in a preliminary stage. Foraging was certainly an important part of their way of life, yet based on all the available evidence it seems reasonable to assume that the Cohonina did practice some agriculture — perhaps "casual horticulture," as Alan Sullivan has recently written me. It seems reasonable that the Cohonina economy was mixed, like their origins. For example, they may have foraged during the cooler months and farmed at least part of the time during the summer. Yet, like the Havasupais, who lived in the same environment hundreds of years later, farming never became the central life theme for the Cohonina that it did for their Anasazi neighbors.

With environmental changes always occurring, and new ideas developing from within and available from the outside, no culture ever remains the same. The Cohonina way of life was no exception. The archaeological record, slim as it is, provides a view of several important changes that took place over the course of 400 years. Cohonina culture can arbitrarily be divided into three phases, beginning with the Coconino phase (A.D. 700 to 900), when they were just beginning their occupation of the region. This was followed by the Medicine Valley phase (A.D. 900 to 1100), the climax of their cultural development, and the Hull phase (post-A.D. 1100). Sometime around the middle of the 1100s, there is no further evidence of Cohonina life.

The earliest date available for the Cohonina culture is A.D. 775, but it is reasonable to assume that it began somewhat earlier. During the Coconino phase, the Cohonina were still mainly foragers, like the earlier Archaic and later Paiute people, living in brush structures, moving seasonally through their territory in small bands, and taking advantage of the resources available at that time. But they had already begun to make pottery, and it is reasonable to assume that very soon after the culture originated they began to farm at least to a limited degree in addition to their hunting and gathering activities, planting and harvesting corn, beans, and squash in favorable locations.

Gradually the population began to increase, and the Cohonina expanded throughout their range. With greater attention given to agriculture, its effects reverberated throughout the culture, affecting their architecture, the kinds of tools they used, and their social and perhaps religious life. In addition to temporary brush shades or jacal structures of poles plastered with mud, they were now also building circular and rectangular one-room pithouses with adjacent pits and rooms for storage.

The Cohonina possessed the full range of tools that would be expected for a self-sufficient group practicing hunting, gathering, and farming, including metates, manos, and mortars, which were used to process wild or domesticated plants. They had distinctively shaped projectile points for tipping arrows and larger spearheads, both used for hunting; stone drills for woodworking; and scrapers and blades for preparing skins.

Their distinctive pottery, San Francisco Mountain Gray ware, although not as well made as that of their Anasazi neighbors, was produced for nearly four centuries. They made a variety of plain and decorated forms, including large jars of up to twenty-five gallons for storing water, smaller jars, and decorated bowls. Like the Anasazi, the Cohonina fired their pottery in a reducing atmosphere, but theirs was less carefully controlled, producing a gray to brown paste. However, in contrast to the Anasazi, who smoothed their coiled pots with a scraper, the Cohonina, as I have said, finished theirs with a paddle and anvil, tying them to potters of the west and south who used the same technique.

From the beginning, Cohonina pottery reflected some aspects of Anasazi ceramic design, as if they had chosen some elements that appealed to them. With slight modifications, Anasazi designs were copied by the Cohonina as long as they made pottery. Their earliest pottery was covered with a fugitive red wash, a practice followed earlier by the Anasazi but discontinued about A.D. 700. Perhaps because the Cohonina did not control their firing as well as the Anasazi or produce a permanent red color, they continued to employ the fugitive red wash for several hundred years.

Cohonina settlements originally were located mainly on the plateau south of the Grand Canyon. Rock shelters in the inner canyon were used only during hunting and gathering expeditions. Seasonally, they probably went into the canyon to find certain foods such as agave, prepared in roasting pits built for that purpose near where they were collected.

Over time, as the population increased, the Cohonina began to settle in the inner canyon. An example of this expansion can be seen at a site found on the north bank of the Colorado River on the Unkar Delta — a small settlement of two structures occupied over a very short period of time about A.D. 900. It consisted of one surface room with low walls of crude limestone masonry and a post-supported roof, along with a very shallow pithouse. Most of the pottery from the structures was Cohonina, although some Anasazi trade pottery of a type known as Deadman's Black-on-red was also found.

What were the Cohonina doing at Unkar Delta? They could have been looking for a new agricultural niche, but no domestic plant remains or pollen were found at either structure, and they might simply have been foraging north of the Colorado River. The settlement was soon abandoned, and apparently the Cohonina never returned to the Unkar Delta, which was not to be settled again until the Anasazi arrived nearly two centuries later.

After A.D. 900, during the Medicine Valley phase, the Cohonina were nearing their peak. Many sites show an intermittent occupation. Possibly the Cohonina moved in and out of the region, depending upon the amount of rainfall. During periods of drought they may have temporarily abandoned a settled existence and returned to foraging, or perhaps these sites were occupied seasonally. However, overall they were becoming more settled, as evidenced by larger and more substantial structures and larger settlements.

For the next three hundred or so years they continued to build temporary shades, but they also built a variety of houses, including main rooms with attached additions, variously called patios or alcoves; long pueblos with several attached rooms; and enigmatic, thick-walled, larger-roomed features called forts. After A.D. 1050 they lived mainly on the plateau and perhaps in Havasu Canyon, but they no longer inhabited other settlements within the Grand Canyon. Their improved building styles, like their pottery designs, may have been borrowed from the Anasazi, but no Cohonina ceremonial structures have been identified, unless that was the function of the "forts."

Not long after A.D. 1100, a major drop in precipitation occurred over the whole northern Colorado Plateau, leading to a drastic decline in the population throughout the region. Over the next century, and perhaps for most of the next fifty years, all of the Cohonina settlements, as well as extensive Anasazi occupations that had also grown up in the area, disappeared.

Just what finally happened to the Cohonina is not clear. Some archaeologists have suggested they remained in the area to become the Havasupais. Others have argued persuasively that after a century or more when there were no settlements in the region, the Cohonina were replaced by a new people, the Cerbat, who moved into the area from the west, and it was they who eventually became the Havasupais. Just how the Cohonina vanished is not made clear in this reconstruction. Thomas Cartledge, of the U.S. Forest Service, has suggested they joined the Anasazi, or "that different Cohonina sub-groups moved off in different directions and affiliated with other groups with whom they had close ties." A third alternative, proposed by Alfred Whiting, suggests that the historic Havasupais were a blend of the older Cohoninas and the later Cerbat, but this does not fit with the 150-year gap in the settlement of the area seen by Robert Euler, an archaeologist with the National Park Service.

So the question of what became of the Cohonina remains as much a mystery as their origins. Yet each year we learn more about these early settlers of the Grand Canyon region — a people who lived throughout their relatively short existence on the edge of economic change, but who were never able to blossom like their Anasazi neighbors.

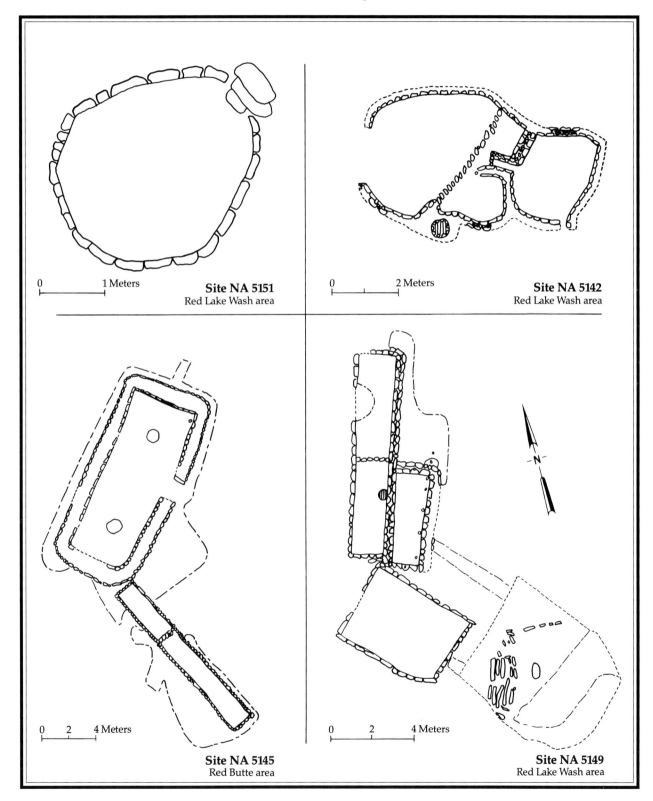

Site NA 5151
Red Lake Wash area

Site NA 5142
Red Lake Wash area

Site NA 5145
Red Butte area

Site NA 5149
Red Lake Wash area

Examples of Cohonina architecture adapted from drawings by D. Schwartz and J. Epstein in John C. McGregor, *The Cohonina Culture of Northwestern Arizona.*

Chapter VI

View of village area in Havasu Canyon. Photo by Douglas W. Schwartz.

Working with the Havasupais

I had only heard about the wonders of this oasis, bordered by red cliffs and cut by a cool, clear, bubbling stream, creating a ribbon of brilliant green in the canyon. This was the traditional summer home of the Havasupai Indians, and for me, the stuff of dreams and adventure.

I first heard about the Havasupais and their canyon home during my work on the Cohonina project in the late 1940s. Thereafter, I became intrigued with the speculation by prominent archaeologists that because the canyon and plateau territory of the prehistoric Cohonina coincided with that of the historic Havasupais, one group may have evolved into the other. During my final undergraduate year at the University of Kentucky and my first two years of graduate work at Yale, the question of the origin of the Havasupais stayed with me, as did a fascination with the Grand Canyon.

And when it came time to choose a topic for my doctoral dissertation, it seemed natural to return to northern Arizona, explore the Havasupais' canyon home, and search for evidence of their prehistoric origins. When I started this project, I had no inkling how far it would lead me intellectually or emotionally, nor of the problems I would encounter undertaking an archaeological project under the constant vigilance of a living community.

With a $1,500 grant from Yale to cover a year's work, I set out enthusiastically (and more than a little naively) from New Haven with my wife, Nita, and our two-year-old son, Steven, expecting to write a new chapter in southwestern history. I planned to set up operations within the village, systematically survey the whole region, record all of its archaeological sites, and then excavate those that might shed light on Havasupai prehistory.

Looking back, I realize how much this work was influenced by my preconception that the prehistoric Havasupais were related to the Cohonina. While I learned a great deal that year about initiating my own research and gained real insight into the life of the Havasupais, it was not until years later that the work taught me the most important lesson a scientist must learn: no matter how good your work or how hard you try, additional research and insights by yourself and others will always supersede earlier conclusions. You must be prepared to give up your hardest-won ideas.

Our first task was to arrange for a Havasupai guide and horses to take us from Peach Springs, south of the canyon, down the treacherous trail with its primitive hairpin turns — the only way into the village. Both Nita and I had considerable experience on horseback, but none on rocky canyon trails. Steven rode on the saddle in front of Nita and was so oblivious to what we saw as a precipitous and dangerous descent that the gentle rocking motion of the horse's gait lulled him to sleep. We, on the other hand, gasped at each turn, and as the trail wound into the canyon's depths, the pressure of the dry, intense heat made us even more anxious.

Finally, the trail led us into the village of Havasu, with the shade of its huge cottonwood trees and the cool of the spring-fed stream. After we took a room at the inn, I found Charlie Wescogomie, the Havasupai friend I had met a few years earlier on the Cohonina project. He introduced me to others, beginning the long and difficult process of obtaining permission to work in the village area. I had not realized that three researchers had already been turned down and that it would take several months of negotiations before I could even start my work. Besides making a presentation to the tribal council and awaiting their deliberations, I had to leave the canyon for most of the winter and obtain permits from the Indian Service office in Phoenix, the Department of the Interior in Washington, the regional National Park Service archaeologists in Santa Fe, and the superintendent of the Grand Canyon National Park. Nothing in my training to this point had prepared me for the bureaucratic aspects of archaeological research.

Finally, the following March, I returned to Havasupai, this time alone and prepared for several months of research. I was able to carry out my survey and discover many archaeological sites, including a series of cliff dwellings overlooking the village. A number of excavations, which

The author's Havasupai guide, near the village of Supai. Photo by Douglas W. Schwartz.

provided new information on Havasupai prehistory, became the basis of my dissertation.

Equally important to my education were the experiences of traveling with a shaman to the edges of Havasupai territory and hearing his stories about the past; playing football with young men in the tribe and being the target of what I sensed were their feelings of frustration and hostility toward the white man; swimming in the pools below the waterfalls and being captured by the magic of the wonderful canyon; and most of all learning, only gradually, the fine line that had to be walked to remain on good terms with the various factions within the village, some of whom were not at all sure what I was doing there.

One of my most memorable experiences at Havasu took place in a sweatbath. My attempts to talk to the shaman had been unsuccessful until I badly turned my ankle and a Havasupai friend arranged for the shaman to sing over me. I was led to the sweatbath, near the stream bank, ushered inside, and sat on the dirt floor between two Havasupai men and the shaman. When a blanket was placed over the door, the small space became pitch black. The shaman began dropping water on a pile of heated cobbles just inside the door. The temperature kept rising, and before long I was woozy from the heat. I slumped lower and lower, trying to get a cooler breath of air, until my nose touched the wet sand. Fortunately, it was too dark for the shaman to see me in this undignified position as he groped for my lower leg, then alternately sang over the ankle and blew on the swollen part.

The formal part of the ritual lasted for about fifteen minutes. I had just started adjusting to the heat when the other two men in the sweatbath began to talk. Weak as I was from the heat, I knew that this was my opportunity to ask the shaman questions which might eventually lead to some understanding of his role in the society. I had almost gathered up enough nerve to speak when he said to me, "How does a man become a priest in the town where you live?" At that moment I knew I had lost the initiative and that he had become the anthropologist.

I did a great deal of growing up within those canyon walls. Isolated geographically and socially, I was forced to learn the standards of another culture both in terms of normal behavior and of what was important in life. I made new friends, although other people simply avoided me. For weeks on end, I tried to think about the past while living in a social system that in many ways seemed opposed to such ways of thinking. Looking back on that time, I probably would do a lot of things differently now. Yet there is no doubt in my mind that I was an extremely lucky young man to have been immersed in the living world of the Havasupais and, at the same time, involved in the search for Grand Canyon prehistory.

People of the Blue Water: The Havasupais

The name *Havasupai* means "the people of the blue water." They live in a canyon threaded by a stream of bluish water, which is fed by a spring that bubbles out of their side canyon, south of the Colorado River. The water emerges from just above their village and runs through it to feed the lush vegetation along the banks of the stream — huge cottonwood trees and thick stands of willows. The stream — Havasu Creek — is also the source of Havasupai irrigation canals, which water their fields of corn, beans, and squash, the most important plants in their summer way of life.

The section of the canyon that holds the village is three miles long and in places only a quarter of a mile wide. Below the village, Havasu Creek tumbles down a series of magnificent falls as it knifes its way through the narrow lower Havasu Canyon, before its clear waters mix with the muddy Colorado River several miles below. The village is about three thousand feet below the rim of the Colorado Plateau, the other home of the Havasupais, an area some ninety by seventy-five miles covered by piñon-juniper forests, grassy meadows, and stands of ponderosa pine. Here in the cooler months they traditionally practiced hunting and gathering to supplement their agricultural harvests.

The split life of the Havasupais, farming in the summer within the canyon and foraging widely during the rest of the year, began in early spring as family groups who had been scattered over the plateau during the winter began moving back into the canyon to clear the debris from the previous year's garden plots and prepare the two hundred or so acres available to them for planting. They also began repairing the irrigation ditches and constructing low dams of earth and brush, which diverted water from the river onto their fields as they were prepared for planting.

In mid-April planting began with the help of juniper digging sticks, with a side branch for a foot rest, and other simple tools. In addition to corn, beans, and squash, the Havasupais farmed domesti-

Havasu Falls. Courtesy Grand Canyon National Park, National Park Service.

cated sunflowers, gourds, and cotton. After the first corn kernel was planted, another would be chewed, then blown toward two white marks on the canyon wall symbolizing the two ancestral ears of corn presented to the Havasupais by their mythical twin culture heros. The plants were then irrigated a few times while some people returned to the plateau to hunt game and collect fresh greens. During the summer the Havasupais returned to the canyon to care for the growing crops, protecting them from rodents and birds by setting traps near the fields, or tethering pet hawks or dogs nearby. The periodic watering and weeding of the fields continued, and as the crops matured and water on the plateau became less available, the Havasupais remained for longer periods near their fields, living in dome-shaped brush huts or in rock shelters overlooking the valley.

Crops began maturing in June and could be harvested through early fall. By that time all crops and many kinds of wild plant foods had been picked and dried for storage. Seeds for the next growing season were also carefully chosen and stored in rock and mud granaries built into the cliffs, out of reach of the damaging floods that occasionally roared through the canyon during violent summer rainstorms.

Havasupai basket makers and home. Courtesy Southwest Museum.

In August, neighboring Hopis, from the east, and Walapais, from the west, were invited to Havasu Canyon for one of the few community-wide ceremonies among the Havasupais, their harvest festival. It was celebrated by feasting, gambling, and trading. A Circle Dance was also held, in which everyone joined hands, faced the center of the circle, and moved in short, sideways steps, expressing and reinforcing their group solidarity.

By the middle of October, their agricultural work completed, the families again returned to the plateau and their scattered, semipermanent camps, from which they would begin once more to range out over the plateau and into the canyon. During this time they gathered piñon nuts, and the seeds, nuts, and fruits of the catclaw, amaranth, shepherd's purse, goosefoot pigweed, tansy mustard, barrel cactus and other kinds of cactus, wild sunflower, mescal, prickly pear, mesquite, and wild grape.

The women, who did most of the gathering, knocked or pulled the seeds from the plants and put them into small collecting baskets. Then they transferred the contents into large, conical carrying baskets, which they packed on their backs to camp. The seeds were dried, toasted, ground, baked, or stored. Food was frequently baked in pits dug in the ground, with a fire built on top. Grains, grasses, cactus, and small game were also parched and boiled.

As winter approached, each family moved up to its traditional camping area on the plateau and built conical huts covered with brush and earth. The men used bows and arrows for hunting, now of primary importance. The best bows, made of ash, were backed with sinew to make them stronger, and the arrows were made of serviceberry or other hard woods, tipped with small stone arrowheads, and feathered from birds raised for that purpose, particularly ferruginous or rough-legged hawks. The arrows were carried in a skin quiver hung over the shoulder.

The Havasupais hunted mainly pronghorn antelope, bighorn sheep, and mule deer, as well as smaller game such as bobcats, rabbits, turkeys, porcupines, quail, doves, and small rodents. They did not have techniques for easily preserving meat, so they usually ate what they had killed in a short period of time. Small hunting parties would go out frequently to keep the camps provided with fresh meat.

The basic Havasupai social group and economic unit was the family. Usually the wife came to live with the husband's close relatives. The group consisted of a man, his wife, their unmarried children, and their married sons and families. Women cared for the children and cooked with wood they collected in the forest, which was also used for heating. Occasionally, a trip would be made back to the canyon to retrieve stored food from the granaries. As the long, cold winters of the plateau came to an end, the cycle of the year would begin again when the Havasupais moved back to the canyon to clear the fields in preparation for planting.

Clothing was usually made from skins. Men wore a shirt, breechcloth, leggins, moccasins, and a headband. Women wore a short under-apron, a long buckskin dress, moccasins, and during periods of cold weather, a rabbitskin blanket. The people wore no elaborate ornamentation except, occasionally, necklaces, earrings, and face paint.

A temporary plateau Havasupai camp. Photo 1936, courtesy Maxwell Museum of Anthropology, University of New Mexico, Albuquerque.

As with the Paiutes, the Havasupais who were recognized as tribal chiefs operated less from any formal authority than from the power conferred on them as a result of the quality of their advice, their persuasive abilities, and their prestige from individual achievement.

The Havasupai cycle of life was not marked by a great deal of ritual. An infant was often painted with red ocher and, at about two weeks of age, tightly bound on a cradleboard, where it spent most of its first year. Young children could play freely around the camps, gradually assuming responsibility for daily chores. Only girls underwent puberty ceremonies. When menstruation started, they were given a special buckskin dress, stained red with powdered ocher. For four days the girl spent most of her time on a bed of sand that had been spread over heated rocks. At sunrise she ran toward the east and at sunset toward the west to ensure she would always perform her work quickly and untiringly. At death the body and most of the person's property was cremated, including their house and all or part of their crops, but there was no formal funeral ceremony.

Religion was not elaborately developed among the Havasupais. They emphasized shamanic rites having to do with healing, weather, and hunting. The shaman's powers were inherited from a former shaman. His spirit, which used the shaman as its medium, came to him in a dream, where he also learned the songs he would use. Leanne Hinton has written that the language of shamanic spirits was thought by the Havasupais to be unintelligible to all human beings except medicine men, dying people, and babies. They believed that the soul left the body during dreams and at death to travel to the land of the dead in the sky. However, some souls remained as ghosts and caused illness and death. Sweatbaths were and still are a popular activity, particularly among the men. Curing songs would be sung in these small, domed wood and dirt structures, helping to solidify the bond between humans and the spiritual power of the universe.

Trade was carried out mainly with the Hopis and Walapais, with whom they traded buckskin, foodstuffs, and basketry for cotton goods, pottery, jewelry, and hides. Beginning in the seventeenth century, the Havasupais began obtaining European trade goods, probably from the Hopis. Foreign items gradually increased in number as the expanding American frontier moved closer. The Havasupais were largely protected from the encounters of frontier warfare by the isolation of their canyon village, and they were one of the last southwestern groups to be heavily influenced by the encroaching culture. By the middle of the nineteenth century, however, cattlemen began taking over their plateau territory and forcing them to concentrate their activities more in the canyon. By the middle of the twentieth century, they were restricted to a 500-acre reservation within the canyon.

With the loss of a major part of their upland foraging grounds, Havasupai life changed radically. Many of their important original campsites such as those around Dripping Spring, where for centuries their ancestors had hunted and gathered, were now lost to them. That part of their old way of life, like that of so many others, was gone.

Although great changes have taken place among the Havasupais, they continue to see the positive aspects of their life. There is still no automobile road to Supai, nor does the tribe ever want to have one, recognizing the value of their relative isolation from the outside world. So the horse and the ancient trails into the canyon remain extremely important to them, as they have been since horses were first introduced by the Spaniards. Horses pack in the mail, supplies, and even some of the healthy flow of tourists, who come to see the beauty of their canyon.

Besides packing and tourism, construction is now an important part of Havasupai income. Over the last few years they have built many of the two- and three-bedroom prefabricated houses in which they now live, as well as two inns, a cafe, a grocery store, and a school teaching kindergarten to eighth grade.

The Havasupais continue to hunt and gather in some of their old lands, mostly on weekends, although now these areas are reached by pickup trucks, which they keep parked at the canyon trailhead. Hunting was made much easier in the late 1970s when their reservation was expanded with the addition of 250,000 acres of their original land, including their waterfalls and much of their traditional wintering lands — the biggest Indian land return in United States history.

So while much of Havasupai life has changed over the past few centuries, their isolation, the beauty of their canyon, and their successful efforts to obtain the rights to their original lands have allowed them more good fortune than many other American Indians. Yet for any group of people, the past is irretrievable. This understanding is reflected in the personal songs of the Havasupais, which express their emotions about each other and life in general. "Farewell Song," collected by linguist Leanne Hinton, evokes the feelings of an old man who had wandered all his life, now too old to travel. Although this song was not intended as an anthem to the end of traditional Havasupai life, it does carry a sense of the many changes that have overtaken the people of the blue water.

Farewell Song

Dripping Spring
land I used to roam,
That place,
Listen to what I say,
Don't mourn for me.
I thought I would be alive forever
I thought I would roam forever,
But here I am
I can't continue on,
Now I am too weak.

Placing hot stones in a sweatlodge. Photo by Terry E. Eiler, 1973.

Chapter VII

Excavations at Unkar Delta, 1967. School of American Research.

Searching for the Canyon Anasazi

By the end of the 1950s there had been several Grand Canyon arch-aeological projects. I had worked on Cohonina sites south of the canyon, completed my doctoral research on Havasupai prehistory, and explored the figurine caves. Ned Hall had carried out a survey on the North Rim, Emil Haury had excavated a site near the South Rim, and a few other smaller surveys had been conducted. But while bits and pieces of the story of Grand Canyon prehistory were beginning to emerge, a systematic program of research to seek out the overall nature of the canyon's human past was missing.

In 1957 I decided to undertake such a program, and for the next twelve years I returned regularly to the canyon to conduct three surveys and four seasons of intensive excavations. This work was designed to gain an understanding of why, how, and when prehistoric people lived in the Grand Canyon region, and how the environment may have changed their way of life. What I did not know at the time was how much of my effort would concentrate on the least-known but most frequent prehistoric inhabitants of the Grand Canyon — the Anasazi.

I chose Shinumo Canyon, a relatively small side canyon in the northwest section of the national park, as the first area for this study. No survey had ever been carried out in a side canyon north of the river, and the area was small enough to conduct a reasonably complete survey despite my limited resources and its relative inaccessibility. Two companions and I descended a trailless fissure from the North Rim into upper Shinumo, our packs loaded with eight days of supplies and equipment, the most we could carry. Below we found a lush, well-watered valley with huge cottonwoods, stands of willows, and rich patches of moss and fern. The water ouzels that dipped below the surface of the creek for minnows led us to believe that the creek flow was permanent, yet the pure desert environment only a few feet away from the water course was murderously hot.

Working our way through the two branches of the canyon, we found twenty-three sites, including small habitation rooms and agricultural terraces and check dams. From the types of pottery we found scattered on the ground, it was clear these sites had been used by Anasazi. The designs on the sherds indicated that the sites had been used sometime between the A.D. 900s and A.D. 1200. After eight days we worked our way back to the North Rim — a backbreaking climb because we were carrying out all the pottery we had found at the sites for later study.

In 1960 I returned for a survey in Nankoweap, a side canyon north of the river, chosen specifically because it was at the other end of the park from Shinumo. My crew included a graduate student assistant; a physician friend interested in archaeology; my wife, Nita, who would do the cooking; our son, Steven, now nine; and our five-year-old daughter, Susan, who was making her first trip into the Grand Canyon. At the time it seemed natural to include my children in this venture, but I did not appreciate its potential dangers.

Douglas W. Schwartz exploring cliff granaries. School of American Research.

From the hard experience of the Shinumo survey, I concluded that a helicopter was the only practical means of transport. No helicopters had yet been used for archaeology in the Grand Canyon, and in fact, they had first been employed there only the year before in the rescue effort after a midair airline collision. The danger of these logistics did not occur to me. Impressed by the romance and efficiency of the helicopter as a means of transportation and eager to have my young family share this experience, I was ruled more by my youthful enthusiasm for getting the job done than by thoughts of safety. A year after the survey was completed, my heart leaped to my throat when I heard that our pilot had been killed when his helicopter crashed.

The Nankoweap project was extremely productive, revealing forty-eight sites: granaries; habitations with from one to six rooms, three with what appeared to be kiva depressions, the first such features found within the canyon; and several apparent agricultural areas. I excavated one room to sample the depth of midden and found it to be extremely shallow, information that was useful a few years later as I planned my first extensive inner-canyon excavations. The pottery showed exactly what I had seen at Shinumo, an exclusively Anasazi occupation that began about A.D. 1050 and was over by A.D. 1200. Sooner than I had expected, a pattern was beginning to emerge for the prehistory of the inner canyon.

Another three years passed, during which time I was carrying out my other project, on the archaeology of Kentucky, before I was able to return to the canyon. Previously I had traveled on foot, on horseback, and by helicopter; this time I would need boats. I was interested in the area between the mouth of Nankoweap Canyon and the place along the river where Granite Gorge began, an area of river ledges and accessible side canyons that could well have been inhabited by prehistoric people.

We again used helicopters to fly in with our gear, which this time included three motorless, one-man inflatable rubber rafts. I planned to float down the river, stopping regularly to survey the river bank or ascend the side canyons to look for prehistoric remains. But the river was much more powerful than I had expected, and in the end we used the boats largely to hold supplies as we pulled them down the river from the bank, or more frequently, over the muddy rocks — a rough way to travel.

In spite of difficulties, the work confirmed what I had seen elsewhere: wherever there was water and arable land, there had once been Anasazi. At the junction of every side canyon and up nearly every creek we found sites — Kwagunt, Lava, Basalt, and a great many on Unkar Delta. For the first time I saw some evidence of use as early as A.D. 900, but here also, the major occupation had occurred during the eleventh and twelfth centuries.

Other archaeologists — Robert Euler, Walter Taylor, George Beck, and Richard Thompson — had also carried out surveys in the canyon region by this time, but I felt the pattern of human settlement was clear enough to justify a major inner-canyon excavation to learn more about the life of these ancient people. So in 1967, with major help from the National Science Foundation, I began a two-year project on Unkar Delta, the location that all my surveying had led me to believe would provide the most information.

To carry out the excavations, it was necessary to transport twenty people and tons of equipment for a seven weeks' stay at the bottom of the canyon. This was a totally new kind of archaeology. No one had ever attempted such an ambitious helicopter-supported expedition, and it was to be the first major excavation within the canyon itself.

In the middle of May we dropped onto Unkar Delta and set up a tent camp. The first two days we were tested severely by the 120-degree heat and high winds that stung us with sand and knocked down every tent. But once the wind died down and we became conditioned to the heat — in part by plunging into the 60-degree waters of the Colorado River at the end of each work day — we began our work in earnest.

We studied the varied ecology of the delta to be in a position to determine how the Anasazi had utilized the inner canyon. During our intensive survey of the delta's 300 acres and up the side canyon leading to the North Rim cliffs, we found over ninety-four sites, several with large rooms and well-made kivas, plus extensive agricultural terrace systems. We planted and tended experimental gardens and observed their progress to gain some insight into the problems of the Anasazi farmers. Also, tree-ring studies revealed that settlements occurred only when there was enough precipitation to sustain life, until the late A.D. 1100s, when a major drought drove the Anasazi from the canyon region.

Douglas W. Schwartz and Robert Wiggs pulling a raft through Kwagunt Rapids, 1961. Photo by Berle Clay.

The North Rim work brought an end to my concentrated search for the prehistory of the Canyon Anasazi. It had been an important time for my family, my children's young lives punctuated time and again by these projects. And it had been a significant time for me as an archaeologist, beginning in small, isolated canyons like Shinumo and moving on to the completion of large research projects. My experiences there led me to appreciate fully the nature of the land in which the Anasazi had lived and the ways they developed to survive, at least for a time, in the beauty and rigor of the Grand Canyon.

The Grand Canyon Anasazi

The dominant presence in the prehistoric Grand Canyon region were the Anasazi. For a time in the A.D. 1000s and 1100s, they seemed to have been everywhere except south and west of the region, areas used by the Cohonina. Well over one thousand Anasazi sites have been found in the canyon area, including rock-lined roasting pits, cliff granaries, agricultural terraces and fieldhouses, rock paintings and petroglyphs, and hundreds of single- to many-room pueblo dwellings.

The Anasazi were the people who built the great structures at Mesa Verde and Chaco Canyon and whose descendants were the Pueblo peoples the Spaniards found living over much of the northern Southwest. By A.D. 600 they were living throughout the Four Corners country, occupying small villages of three to twenty pithouses, and making pottery for cooking and storage, as well as a wide range of stone and wooden tools. They lived by farming maize, beans, and squash, supplemented by gathering and hunting.

Gradually the Anasazi expanded beyond their original heartland, some moving west over the Little Colorado River, first appearing in the Grand Canyon region about A.D. 700. For the first few hundred years they may have moved in seasonally, using the area only sparingly and intermittently, mainly for foraging. Then about A.D. 1050, when pressure was being exerted from an increasing population to the east and favorable moisture conditions allowed farming to be practiced profitably in the area, the canyon region exploded with Anasazi settlements. Soon the Anasazi spread widely over the landscape, from the South Rim plateau, to hundreds of locations deep within the canyon itself, to the Kaibab Plateau to the north, and even to the tops of remote pillars of rock standing apart from the rimrock with romantic names like Sky Island and Wotan's Throne.

For 150 years after A.D. 1050, the Anasazi moved in and out of the region in response to changes in moisture, for, like their contemporary Cohonina neighbors, they depended on favorable environmental conditions for their economic existence. When there was more precipitation — and even a slight amount seems to have made a difference — they established settlements. What happened when moisture levels declined is not as clear, beyond the fact that they abandoned their communities. They may have moved out of the region for a time or stayed, reverting back to a foraging way of life.

The most extensive research on the Canyon Anasazi, carried out on Unkar Delta, revealed three main periods of occupation (presented in the figure below), each related to a time of higher precipitation. After

View of Unkar Delta from Sky Island on the North Rim. School of American Research.

these occupations, the Anasazi permanently abandoned the inner canyon. A final phase of occupation on the South Rim is known from the excavation of a well-made pueblo called Tusayan Ruin.

Farmers Need Water

The hot, dry environment of the inner Grand Canyon is marginal for agriculture, and the North Rim plateau is so cool that it has only a short growing season. So for prehistoric farmers to survive outside the well-watered Havasupai Canyon, there had to be exactly the right combination of moisture and temperature, a condition that did not often or regularly occur.

The archaeological record clearly reveals a pattern of intermittent settlement broken by periods of no observable occupation. Based on the tree-ring record, which reveals the changing levels of moisture during the prehistoric period, farming settlements existed in the Grand Canyon region only when moisture levels were above normal.

This close relationship between high levels of precipitation and the presence of settlements can best be seen on Unkar Delta, where the most extensive research has been carried out. The pattern of settlement broken by times of no settlement evident there probably reflects what was happening throughout the region during the farming period, not only to the Anasazi, but to the Cohonina as well.

Unkar Delta was occupied for relatively short periods around A.D. 900, just after A.D. 1050, and prior to and following A.D. 1100. No settlements were found dating to the intervening periods, which had lower levels of moisture. The later settlement at Tusayan Ruin, near the South Rim, also occurred during a short period of slightly increased precipitation.

As archaeological research continues in the region, it will be possible to refine even further this critical tie between moisture, farming, and settlement. Perhaps we will also discover what happened to the Anasazi between the periods of settlement.

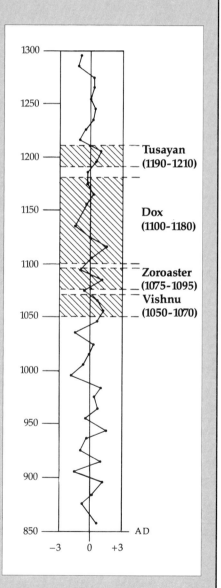

Periods of Anasazi occupation in the Grand Canyon region superimposed on a curve of hypothetical changes in precipitation.

The Vishnu Phase

The first period of Anasazi settlements for which we have good evidence lasted no more than two decades during a time of increased precipitation. These early settlements were built around pithouses and above-ground shades, or ramadas. Already, the people had the full range of tools and utensils necessary to lead essentially self-sufficient lives.

During this time the Anasazi used the plateau south of the canyon and east to the territory of the Cohonina, who were gradually moving west. They also were beginning to use the inner canyon and the forests of the North Rim.

Our best view of life during this time comes from what I will call the Sullivan site, excavated by Alan Sullivan of the University of Cincinnati and located just south of the canyon's rim in Kaibab National Forest. This small settlement is important for several reasons: the comprehensive way in which it was excavated; the extent to which its contents were preserved; and the circumstances surrounding its destruction.

The Sullivan settlement consisted of one shallow pithouse and three ramadas, each with its own hearth. At 6,700 feet in elevation, it lies in an extensive piñon-juniper woodland with an understory of sage and little surface water close by. The woods were rich in mule deer, jackrabbits, cottontails, and smaller mammals, and many wild plants and occasional crops of nutritious piñon nuts were available.

The pithouse was built by digging a shallow pit and leveling the floor with stone covered with a thick layer of clay. Masonry walls were built on this base, bound by thick layers of clay and faced with mud. A plaster-lined hearth was placed in the southwest part of the floor. The whole was covered with a roof of beams containing a smokehole over the hearth.

The three nearby ramadas were made of wood and brush. Their floors were also placed in a shallow pit covered with clay and containing a central hearth. Partial walls were made of two or three horizontally laid logs held in place by vertically set posts, the upper walls probably made of brush, branches, and bark covered with dirt. Four upright corner posts served as the base of a roof.

Around and within these structures were found a variety of pottery objects, large cooking jars, pitchers, small jars and bowls, a range of chipped-stone tools, and two corncobs. Scrapers made of antler and some processed yucca fibers were also found; the latter may be the remains of yucca twine used in the construction of a basket. Manos and handstones in the ramadas may have been used to crack open piñon nuts found stored in the jars with prickly pear fruits.

Corn had been stored in two of the ramadas, although no pollen of corn, beans, or squash was found during the excavation, suggesting that farming was not carried out near the village, but somewhere more favorable to agriculture. Other wild-food remains were present, all well known to the Pueblo people, including charred seeds of pigweed and goosefoot. And in an area outside the masonry pithouses, pottery had been made and fired.

Artist's conception of Anasazi climbing to the top of Wotan's Throne. Illustration by Robert W. Nicholson.

In the summer of A.D. 1064, after about fifteen years of occupation, this small Anasazi village was suddenly and catastrophically destroyed, probably by a forest fire. What remained after the fire, which left so many everyday artifacts in place, has provided us with a rare view of life in a small outpost of Anasazi culture at the beginning of their Grand Canyon occupation.

We know from excavations I carried out that a similar way of life was practiced within the Grand Canyon at pithouse settlements on Unkar Delta, the largest arable area at river level in the canyon, and at Bright Angel Delta, further downstream. Unkar Delta and other parts of the inner canyon had been used for a short time by the Cohonina a century and a half earlier, and when precipitation increased, it became possible for the Anasazi to farm there.

So while the Anasazi had obviously used the canyon region for many centuries, the first evidence of settling down began about A.D. 1050. The North Rim may also have been used during this early period, but no pithouses or other habitations have been found there, and it is reasonable to assume that serious occupation of the Kaibab Plateau did not begin until later. The end of this tentative probing of the region by the Anasazi probably coincided with a drop in precipitation that made farming impossible and perhaps made even foraging difficult.

The Zoroaster Phase

A revolutionary change in Anasazi settlement began about A.D. 1075 in the Grand Canyon region. Following an abandonment of perhaps a decade, probably caused by a short drought of the kind that so frequently affected life in this marginal area, the Anasazi appear to have poured back into the region in much greater numbers. Now, rather than small, temporarily occupied pithouses, they constructed well-planned, above-ground pueblos consisting of several rooms, and for the first time they built ceremonial kivas near their habitations — one indication that they were committed to year-round communal occupation. They also exploited a much wider range of the region's varied environments and for the first time probably farmed on the Kaibab Plateau.

During the Zoroaster phase the Anasazi spread rapidly throughout the canyon region, occupying nearly every arable area that was not part of Cohonina territory. Their architecture changed dramatically. On Unkar Delta the number of rooms increased from the two of the previous period to twenty-three, suggesting a corresponding increase in population, and the people seem to have lived there year round. On the basis of the number of fire hearths, the community was composed of approximately ten families.

But in addition to the increase in the number of rooms and the apparent permanency of the population, the style of architecture was radically different. Instead of being dug into the ground, the habitations were made of stone and built above ground in regular blocks of two to seven contiguous rooms, forming either a single continuous line or a U shape around a plaza. In two of the plazas they built square subterranean kivas, a feature still used by Pueblo Indians for ceremonial purposes.

The coursed masonry of these pueblos was laid in adobe mortar to form the lower half of the walls. The upper portions were probably built with small logs and interwoven brush, which would have been well suited to the canyon heat, providing shade and allowing the circulation of any cooling breezes. The roofs were of beams and poles covered with a light layer of adobe, and the floors were prepared with an adobe finish. Storage space was provided by pits that had been dug below the floor.

In contrast to the first Anasazi use of the canyon, it is now quite clear that agriculture was an important economic activity. Pollen of corn, squash, and beans and the remains of corncobs were found during the excavation of these sites. Although foraging must also have been carried on to supplement the farming, little evidence of hunting was found.

The stone artifacts found during the excavations show a wide complement of tools — manos and metates for processing domesticated and wild plants, axes and drills for working with wood, arrow points for hunting, and scrapers for preparing skins. Pottery was also made at these sites, judging from the presence of polishing stones and ceramic scraping tools, although pottery may also have been carried in by newly arriving settlers or traded in throughout the occupation.

Ponderosa pine grasslands on the North Rim. Photo 1969 by Karl Kernberger. School of American Research.

Expansion to the North Rim

Sometime during the latter half of the eleventh century, the Anasazi expanded to the Kaibab Plateau to farm, but the change is more likely to have occurred a quarter of a century later during the Zoroaster phase. Besides farmland, the plateau gave the Anasazi a place to escape the oppressive heat of the canyon summer. They may also have been able to multiply their yields by planting early in the warm canyon, then farming on the plateau during its short summer season, and even planting a

second, later crop in the canyon, given the extreme length of the growing season there.

Hundreds of small Anasazi fieldhouses have been found on the North Rim, mostly concentrated near the heads of trails leading between the plateau and the inner canyon. Apparently from their canyon settlements, the Anasazi hiked onto the North Rim and established agricultural fields near the trailhead. The North Rim was probably used only in the summer. Deep snow and cold probably made winter habitation impossible, although the Anasazi may have hunted there in the fall.

Most of the North Rim sites were small fieldhouses, many with associated artificial rock terraces, garden plots, or check dams, clearly used in connection with agricultural activities. Such features improved yield by retaining soil moisture or replenishing the soil by capturing rain-washed silt. Small tributary arroyos were also dammed to divert runoff into adjacent gardens. Pollen samples taken from rooms and from behind the terraces indicate that corn, beans, and squash were all being grown here.

The fields were located carefully, for on the Walhalla Plateau the Anasazi were pushing the upper limits of their ability to farm. They planted on the upper slopes of hills or on the relatively flat tops of ridges, which would be warmed by air rising from the inner canyon. Conversely, they avoided placing fields in the plateau's valley bottoms, where the plants could have been harmed by the cooler air draining through.

The small fieldhouses were made of the local Kaibab limestone. One or two rooms were the norm, although occasionally up to four were placed together. They were covered by a simple roof of beams and poles and had a hard-packed earthen floor. Few of these rooms contained fire hearths or many other features, suggesting that they were used by a few people for a short period of time while the fields were being tended, and then these structures were used during the winter to store the harvested crops or seeds for the following year.

The Anasazi settled throughout the canyon and appeared to be aggressively pushing their occupation in all directions, but shortly before A.D. 1100, precipitation levels fell below what was required to support farming, and the people abandoned the area rapidly. Once again, this was only to be a temporary departure.

The Dox Phase

In the early A.D. 1100s, the canyon area was settled once again. Only a short time had passed since the previous settlement, but important changes are evident in how the Anasazi used the inner canyon, the nature of their architecture, and the styles of their tools. Most notably, instead of pueblos laid out in regular lines or U shapes, they now built heterogeneous complexes of contiguous and noncontiguous features, and no sites seemed to include more than two habitation rooms. On Unkar Delta, only one kiva has definitely been identified from this period, perhaps pointing to a population of a single integrated social unit. All of this suggests a much different sense of what was important in constructing a community, as if a different Anasazi were settling Unkar Delta, a people who possessed a changed view of how their world should be ordered.

Bright Angel Pueblo is an example of a number of more isolated Dox settlements throughout the Grand Canyon. Near the Bright Angel Trail, just north of the suspension bridge across the Colorado River, it can easily be visited by hikers. The pueblo was built at the site of an earlier pithouse but begun about four decades later (A.D. 1100), when the Dox settlement was forming on Unkar Delta. Three surface masonry rooms were built in a single line along the talus slope. The original habitation included a living room with hearth, a living or storage room, and a partially

Bright Angel Ruin. School of American Research.

walled and roofed work area. In a plaza area, facing the rooms, a subterranean pit structure was built with a ventilator to the east and a central slab-lined hearth and ash pit — probably a kiva.

About A.D. 1100, after what appears to have been a short abandonment, sites on the Walhalla Glades declined significantly, never again reaching the earlier numbers even when precipitation levels rose early in the 1100s. Nevertheless, life there continued much as it had earlier. However, one-room sites were seldom built, and two- or three-room structures became more common, suggesting that agriculture was now concentrated in fewer locations.

In the Walhalla Glades section of the North Rim after A.D. 1100, structures were built quite differently from anything constructed previously. Walhalla Ruin, which can also be visited, is just off the road near Cape Royal, on a ridgetop in an open ponderosa pine forest about 150 meters from the rim of the canyon. Here four large rooms were constructed in a line, and adjacent to them on the west are two small, noncontiguous rooms parallel to the main block. Trash around the rooms suggests the settlement was occupied for a considerable period of time.

Four adult human skeletons were found here, two males and two females, buried on their right sides in semiflexed positions, and all with pottery. Three of the bodies had been laid in shallow pits dug through floors, and the fourth was buried in the fill outside a room.

Downstream from Awatobi Creek, 1961. Photo by Douglas W. Schwartz.

Excavating a corrugated pot, Unkar Delta, 1968. Photo by John MacGregor.

Pottery from Walhalla Glades. Photo by George H. H. Huey, 1989.

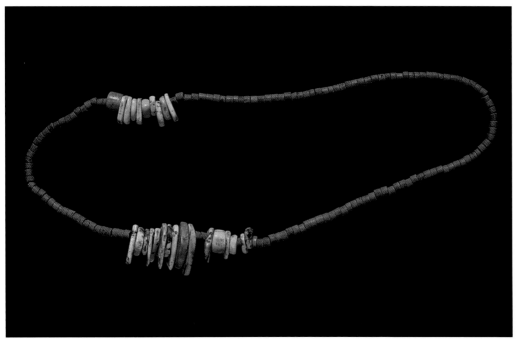

Bracelet found in burial at Walhalla site GC 212. Photo 1969 by Douglas W. Schwartz.

A younger male was buried with two bowls and three jars. A bowl had been inverted over the mouth of a jar, perhaps to protect water placed there to accompany the body into future life. One of the females wore a wonderful wrist bracelet: 139 tiny beads of a shale-like material and 27 turquoise beads and pendants (also see color photograph).

All of these burials were accompanied by pottery of the Flagstaff Black-on-white type, suggesting they were interred sometime after A.D. 1175. These burials appear to have been among the last events to have taken place at the site, so it seems these North Rim settlements continued into the final quarter of the century.

The most fascinating of the North Rim sites were built on Sky Island and Wotan's Throne, two rock pillars standing away from the plateau. The smaller of these, Sky Island, separated from the plateau by only a few hundred meters, held by far the largest site discovered on the Walhalla Glades. Most of its eighteen masonry rooms were quite small, and only one hearth was found, indicating the site may have been a combined facility for storage, food processing, and temporary habitation.

On Wotan's Throne, a much larger rock island some distance off the North Rim, a few crude, room-like structures were found along with two cliff granaries and what was possibly a rough agricultural terrace. The isolation of both of these pillars may have enhanced the protection of stored food, although we have no indication that a defensible location was important to the people of Walhalla Glades.

About A.D. 1180 there may have been another interruption of Anasazi occupation in the Grand Canyon area during a sharp decline in precipitation, but by the middle of the century the climate had improved enough to allow life to continue as it had before. However, between A.D. 1175 and 1200 the Anasazi occupation of the North Rim and the inner canyon again appears to have come to end, and except for a short burst of settlement a few years later on the South Rim, this marked the final chapter in the major habitation of the canyon region.

The Tusayan Phase

Tusayan Ruin was the final Anasazi settlement in the Grand Canyon area. Fifteen miles east of Grand Canyon Village on the main South Rim road, it too can be visited. Tusayan Pueblo was occupied during a relatively wet period between A.D. 1190 and 1209, following the inner canyon and North Rim abandonments. However, there were no settlements within the canyon at this time, as there had been during previous periods of higher precipitation.

Tusayan Pueblo consisted of about eight one-story masonry rooms, all arranged around a U-shaped plaza. It also had two kivas, one part of the main cluster of rooms and the other a few feet south of the east wing.

The excavations of Tusayan Ruin were carried out during the 1930s, and not enough information was obtained to fully describe the life of its inhabitants. But it was obviously an important habitation, and presumably the base for a full Anasazi agricultural community. The pueblo was considerably larger than the early Anasazi habitations on

Pots from burial at Walhalla Ruin. School of American Research.

the South Rim, consistent with the pattern that, over time, Anasazi sites in the Grand Canyon were becoming larger and fewer in number.

Like their predecessors in the Grand Canyon area, the Anasazi of Tusayan Ruin were pushed and pulled by complementary forces. They were pushed, at least in part, by increasing population in their heartland to the east as a result of temporarily improved environmental conditions. And they were pulled toward unused marginal land by the perennial optimism of pioneers hoping to discover a territory for permanent settlement.

When the Tusayan Pueblo was abandoned, all Anasazi occupation in the Grand Canyon region came to an end. But their use of the canyon for ritual purposes was far from over.

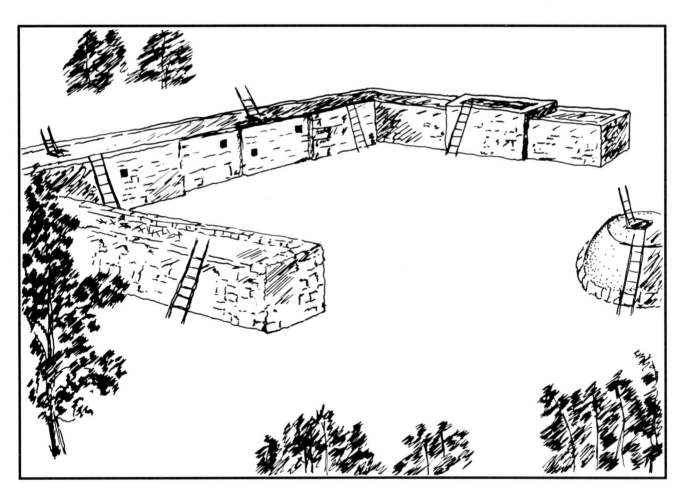

Reconstruction of Tusayan Ruin. Drawing by Katrina Lasko.

Chapter VIII

Hopi sipapuni, on the Little Colorado River, 1961. Photo by Douglas W. Schwartz.

Hiking to the Sipapuni

It seemed completely out of place, this yellowish-brown dome of rock on the bank of the Little Colorado River, rimmed by sheer red cliffs. Yet there it was in front of me, the sacred sipapuni of the Hopis, the formation out of which their ancestors had ascended into this world.

Just a week earlier, our helicopter had landed on the bank of the Colorado River, near the mouth of Nankoweap Creek, to deposit the three of us, our gear, and the three one-man inflatable rafts we would use to travel down the river as far as Unkar Delta. It was one of the early trips that had been made by helicopter into the canyon and the first in support of archaeological research. Only a few years had passed since a TWA passenger plane had gone down in the canyon and helicopters had made the first flights in as part of the rescue.

I had already conducted archaeological surveys in Havasu and Shinumo canyons in the western part of the park and Nankoweap Canyon in the eastern part, and a pattern of prehistoric occupation was beginning to take shape for me. My objective now was to see how the land along the river might have been used during prehistoric times.

It was June 1965. There were very few river runners at this time, and during the whole of the next two weeks we saw no other boats. The rafts were intended to carry our supplies and equipment and make it easier to survey the banks, but I had not counted on how difficult it would be to traverse the rapids in these little boats. So we spent much of the time lining them along the shore and only occasionally trusting our luck to running the river.

The high cliffs downstream from Nankoweap showed no signs of prehistoric use, but as soon as we reached Kwagunt Canyon and hiked to near its headwaters, I found the same pattern of settlement I had seen elsewhere north of the river, the remains of Anasazi occupation. On the basis of the designs on the pottery sherds scattered over the ground surface, the rooms dated from about A.D. 1050 to 1150.

By the fifth day we had reached the mouth of the Little Colorado River. It was just as spectacular as I had heard it would be. Into the raging brown waters of the Colorado flowed this calm, narrow, strikingly beautiful stream of bluish-white water, the effluent from the Little Colorado.

The day was quite hot by the time we arrived at the junction, but we could not miss this rare opportunity to visit something quite special. With a canteen of water, a camera, and a notebook, we walked into the narrow gorge between high cliffs and followed the small river upstream as it meandered back and forth across the canyon. We spent most of our time wading through the bluish water, giving us ample time to observe what seemed to be a white coating under the water, covering the rocks and the river bottom.

The hike seemed endless in the heat. The sun beat down on us from a cloudless sky, and the reflection from the cliff walls made it even hotter. But when we finally reached our destination, it was well worth the effort.

For suddenly, there in front of us, was the origin place of a people — as sacred to the Hopis as Bethlehem to the Christians, Mecca to the Moslems, and Benares to Hindus.

We circled the dome, trying to understand its geological structure: a travertine or similar formation produced by the mineral content of an artesian spring that for ages had poured onto the dome, slowly increasing its height. Climbing to the top over its slightly loose, grainy surface, we found in the center of the dome the pool of bubbling yellowish water through which the ancestors of the Hopis had emerged into this world. The sanctity of the spot affected us all, and for much of the time we were there we spoke very little.

Junction of the Colorado and Little Colorado rivers. Courtesy Grand Canyon National Park, National Park Service.

The Canyon Anasazi
and Hopi Religion

Where did the Anasazi go after they had struggled for two centuries to survive the rigors of the Grand Canyon? Judging from limited archaeological evidence and clues from mythology and religion, it is reasonable to suggest that when they left the canyon they moved east and became part of the ancestral line of the Hopi Indians, profoundly influencing the development of Hopi cosmology.

In the 1600s the Spaniards found the Hopis living in a string of settlements south of Black Mesa and east of the Little Colorado River in what later became northeastern Arizona. Their towns were composed of one- and two-story apartment-like dwellings of stone and mortar arranged around plazas containing ceremonial kivas. The people were organized into independent clans, cross-cut by a number of religious societies with an extremely complex ceremonialism and rich cosmological lore.

The Hopi economy was based on a communally organized agriculture, which depended largely on the dry farming of corn, beans, squash, and cotton. Rain was of critical importance for the success of their crops because of the arid environment in which they lived, and water, from both rain and snow, became the focus of their ceremonial life. The picture of Hopi life then fits precisely with what we know of the life way of the Canyon Anasazi.

The Hopis were descendants of the Anasazi, who possessed a Pueblo culture and who had lived for centuries throughout northern Arizona. In the A.D. 1100s, the ancestral Hopis lived in small pueblos and isolated farmsteads. From then until the 1300s, these early Hopi settlements grew to between 500 and 1,000 people as they were joined by Anasazi from the surrounding areas, bringing with them ideas of their own about cosmology, ritual, and religion. That many of these ideas were added to Hopi life is seen in the variety of their myths: each Hopi settlement has stories of its own, not exactly like those told in the other villages.

The devastating drought that began about A.D. 1150 ultimately forced the Canyon Anasazi to look elsewhere for a place to rebuild their lives. They had originated from Anasazi to the east and maintained a

Shrine, Hopi, Arizona, ca. 1910.
Courtesy Museum of New Mexico,
negative no. 21609.

A Hopi village, ca. 1900. Kenneth M. Chapman Collection, School of American Research.

consistent trading relationship with them, which meant the Canyon Anasazi were well aware that farming was still possible to the east. Those who did not die of malnutrition in the early years of the drought probably migrated east to rejoin their cultural cousins across the Little Colorado River in the area of the Hopi mesas, just about the time Oraibi and other early ancestral Hopi settlements were forming.

This migration of Canyon Anasazi and other Anasazi people may be one source of the legend that during the early years of its ancestral development, many clans came together to form the Hopi tribe, as retold in Peter Whiteley's *Bacavi: Journey to Reed Springs:*

It was Maasaw, guardian of this fourth world [who told the earliest Hopis] that the people would leave this place separately and go off on migrations to the four ends of the earth. Then, a few at a time over a long period, they would return to dwell in his domain at *Tuwanasavi*, the earth's center. They would build a settlement near this place, its name to be "Oraibi."

With widespread drought driving so many people to seek admission to the Hopi communities, substantial pressure must have been applied to the original settlers. It is reasonable to assume, therefore, that Hopi leaders would have developed some means for determining which of the new people could join them, a sense of which can be obtained in a legend from the Third Mesa Hopi village of Bacavi:

Gradually, Oraibi grew through the addition of other clans completing their migrations. . . . Admission to the village was not an easy matter. The clan had to prove its worth to the *Kikmongwi* [village chief]. First, the clan leader had to formally request that his people be given permission to move into the village. he *Kikmongwi* questioned him: What benefit did his people have to offer the community? So the clan leader would recount their migrations, indicating that they had been able to survive and endure through the aid of powerful spirits. Moreover, many clans owned a ceremony which, with the help of their protecting spirits, could benefit mankind and the whole world. The ceremony could bring rain for the crops and health and fertility for the people, and could provide happiness and entertainment. So the *Kikmongwi* proceeded to ask for a demonstration. If the ceremony proved successful, the clan was invited to move into Oraibi . . . and Oraibi prospered, soon becoming a thriving community. (Peter Whiteley, *Bacavi: Journey to Reed Springs*).

Like many other groups, the Canyon Anasazi probably mixed into early Hopi society and culture, contributing their share of rites and deities to Hopi religion. For historically, references to the Grand Canyon as a sacred place are woven throughout Hopi cosmology and ceremonial practices. The reconstruction of the religion of any prehistoric culture is difficult, at best, but suggestions of what impact the Grand Canyon Anasazi may have made on the Hopis can be found in four separate but related areas: the Hopi myth of emergence, their deity Maasaw, their journey to the earth's navel, and some of their customs associated with death.

Hopi corn growing on dunes below the villages. Photo from Emry Kopta Collection, courtesy Museum of Northern Arizona.

The Myth of Emergence

The Hopis believe their ancestors lived in three previous worlds before coming to this one. In turn, each world had been overcome by chaos and moral decay, forcing their leaders to search for a new world in which to carry on their lives. A bird was therefore dispatched to fly through a hole in the dome-shaped sky and find a fourth world and its owner to request permission to enter. The bird found Maasaw, who allowed the Hopis to move up to his land. To make the migration, they planted a reed, which grew tall enough to pierce the sky of the third

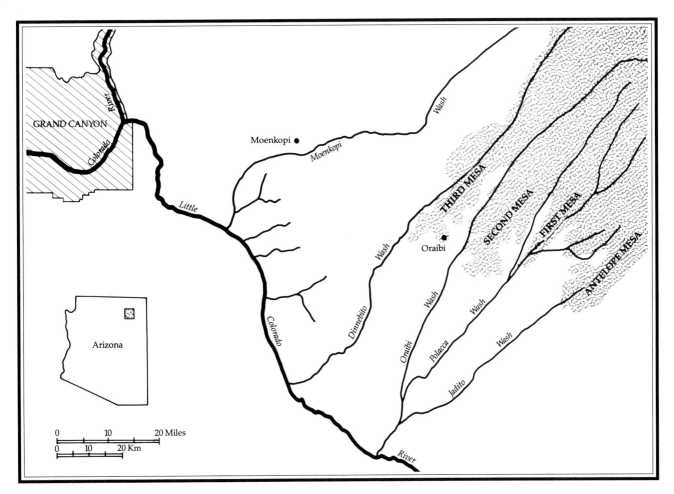

Hopi Mesas. Drawing by Katrina Lasko.

world and create an entrance into the fourth. This entrance was forever after called the sipapuni, the navel. Using the reed as a ladder, the Hopi ascended through the sky, and with the help of Maasaw, climbed through the sipapuni into their peaceful, fresh new world.

The sipapuni out of which the Hopi emerged is a well-known, revered, and until recently, regularly visited place, a flat-topped, dome-shaped geological formation, twenty feet high and thirty feet in diameter. Deep within the Grand Canyon, it lies a few miles up the canyon of the Little Colorado River from its confluence with the Colorado River. In the center of the dome is a pool of yellow bubbling water, through which the original Hopi emerged.

The Hopi Deity Maasaw

Hopi religion involves spirits of animate and inanimate objects, some of which appear as masked personages called kachinas. Other spirits who figure prominently in legends and rituals are considered deities. They are so powerful that they are not impersonated like the kachinas, and many are not even represented by images.

Maasaw, a central figure in Hopi religion, is one of the most powerful and omnipresent of these deities. A god of both life and death, he has a double form, appearing either as a handsome youth or as a grotesque, repulsive, bloody, skeletal creature with large, open eye holes and mouth. Yet Maasaw is "one who lives unseen," so his exact form is not known.

Maasaw was the sole inhabitant and owner of this world, and the "head chief" of the Grand Canyon. Long before the Hopis arrived, he lived near the sipapuni within the canyon. Maasaw gave the Hopis permission to enter his land after they agreed to follow his rules and lead a simple, Spartan, harmonious way of life like his own: "All I own is a planting stick, some seeds, a canteen of water, and a tattered piece of wrap . . . [If] you can live in poverty as I do, you may stay here with me." After the Hopis agreed to his requirements, Maasaw created fire for them to provide the warmth and light necessary for their life. He also gave them their animals and crops.

In the beginning Maasaw did not allow the Hopis to stay with him, but directed that groups of people travel across the land in different directions with the understanding that only later would they return to meet him again, at which time he would give them permission to settle on his land. After the Hopis returned from their migrations, they looked to Maasaw for the fertility of their crops and the health of their animals. Each Hopi farmer planted a portion of his field for Maasaw in his capacity as fertility god.

Journey for Salt

The place of the Grand Canyon in the lives of the Hopis is also interwoven with a salt collecting trip traditionally made each year as part of the ceremonial calendar. The Hopi year begins in November with the celebration of the Wuwuchim ceremony, when a new fire is made and the life of the year is initiated. The ceremony includes a

Quoqole kachina, ca. 1960. School of American Research acquisition from Henry S. Galbraith, 1989.

symbolic enactment of the original emergence from the underworld. The whole ritual is thought of as an offering to Maasaw.

During Wuwuchim young men are made eligible, through initiation, to visit the home of the dead and prepare to take their rightful place in the afterworld. But this initiation is not completed until they journey into the Grand Canyon on the expedition for salt. Fortunately, we have a detailed record of one of these journeys in Don Talayesva's autobiography, *Sun Chief*, which is summarized below.

In the fall, after the harvest, the initiates travel with a group of elders on an arduous trip of several days, traveling west into the Grand Canyon and the sacred land of the dead. After passing Moenkopi, across the Little Colorado River, and the plateau to the west, the travelers climb into the canyon of the Little Colorado, carefully and piously working their way toward the Colorado River, near where they will find the salt cave. On the way they visit a shrine to Spider Woman, who created the salt they will collect, and simulate sexual intercourse with her to ensure an easy journey. They also stop at the shrine of the Twin War gods, her grandchildren and protectors of the Hopis and their land. It was the Twins who established the rules for a safe journey to the salt.

Further into the canyon they come to the cave home of Maasaw and offer prayers that reflect the power he is felt to possess: "Great Masau'u, accept our gifts and grant us a smooth path and an easy journey. Send rain so that our people may live in plenty without sickness, and sleep in old age." They later visit the house of the Muddy Head kachinas and pray again for rain and "strong lives."

The focus of this journey is their visit to the original sipapuni, the place of emergence. Arriving at its dome of rock, they remove their moccasins "before entering the sacred place" and climb to the top. The War Chief shouts, "At last we are here!" and "The spirits answered, for the yellowish water bubbled up as if it were boiling." Prayer sticks are placed on the edge of the hole, and a path of corn meal is sprinkled toward the east — "the main road that the Six-Point-Cloud-People travel when they emerge from the sipapuni to bring rain to the Hopi."

While many Hopi rituals are connected with rain, this one directly ties the rain that falls on Hopi fields to the Grand Canyon sipapuni. For it is from here that the Cloud People "ascend into the air, look eastward, and go to the farms of the most worthy people." Also, only at the sipapuni can the group collect the special yellowish clay that they use for making prayer sticks for the winter solstice ceremony, Soyal.

The party then continues to the junction of the Little Colorado and the Colorado rivers, where they pray again and deposit prayer feathers. Here they also dip their hands into the river and throw water toward their village four times, "encouraging the Cloud People to hasten to [their] homes with rain." After a drink from "the sacred river," they continue to the cave where they collect salt. Once this is completed they can begin their return home, traveling back through the canyon that is sacred to them as the place of Hopi birth and a place where rain originates.

Death

After death the Hopis of Third Mesa are buried facing west toward the canyon and the setting sun. Their faces are covered with a cotton mask, which transforms their departed spirits into clouds, the form in which the dead regularly return to "drop rain upon [the Hopis'] parched lands" (Henry R. Voth, "Four Hopi Tales"). After spending four days in the grave, their breath bodies "travel to the Grand Canyon home of Maasaw, where they are met by sentinels from the Kwan society, who are associated with Maasaw, and either allowed to proceed or punished in fire pits for non-Hopi behavior until they are purified" (Fred Eggan, "The Hopi Indians").

In a Third Mesa legend, Maasaw describes his role in death: "I make sure that whoever dies comes to reside in my home down below ... anyone who dies with a pure heart will come to me. As soon as he does, I'll welcome him and take him to the opening of a kiva [the original sipapuni in the canyon] from where I send him down to the underworld to another life." (Ekkehart Malotki and Michael Lomatuway'ma, *Hopi Coyote Tales*). The spirits of the dead then live in bliss in the underworld, where they are not obliged to engage in the hard work that characterized their lives as farmers.

Hopi women are instructed not to dispose of their wedding robes during their lifetime; after death they will use them as vehicles to descend to the underworld. The robe is not embroidered because it would make it too heavy to be ridden by the dead woman when she was traveling to the land of the dead, her final resting place, deep below the Grand Canyon.

Just as Maasaw takes part in the death of individuals, so he will attend the future death and renewal of Hopi society. Present at the beginning of this world, the fourth, he said, "I'm the first." And from his home in the Grand Canyon, on the last day of existence, it will be Maasaw who oversees the travels of the Hopis to the next world: "I'm also going to be the last."

Thoughts on Hopi Religion

Clearly, the Grand Canyon plays an important role in Hopi cosmology and mythology. But from the present evidence it is impossible to say whether the ancestral Anasazi-Hopis already had these ideas before the Anasazi moved into the Grand Canyon, or if parts of these myths were early aspects of Hopi religion — such as the emergence story or Maasaw — and the Canyon Anasazi only added the location to the story. Or perhaps none of the traits in Hopi religion relating to the sacredness of the Grand Canyon came with the Canyon Anasazi, but were added at a later time.

Presently we cannot say which of these alternatives or what combination of them might be true, and given the abstract nature of religion, we may never discover what happened. Still, buried in the few bits of knowledge we do have, several clues lead me to an appealing if not completely defensible hypothesis that at least serves as a way of thinking about the development of Hopi religion.

Hopi woman carrying her wedding garments. Museum of Northern Arizona Collection.

I would propose that the early religion of the Anasazi ancestors of the Hopis included neither Maasaw nor kachinas. Then sometime in the late A.D. 1100s, as a result of a deepening drought, Anasazi from many religions left their parched homes and joined the Hopi cousins. Each group brought with them religious ideas, ceremonies, and ideas relating directly to the Grand Canyon. Once accepted, these ceremonies were performed, like many of the earlier Anasazi religious practices, during the fall and winter. Somewhat later, perhaps in the 1300s and 1400s, a new group of ceremonies and spiritual figures came to the Hopis from the south — the kachinas and their related cult activities. Unlike the deities that had been brought to the Hopis from the region of the Grand Canyon, the kachinas became active and appeared to them only during the spring and summer, retreating south to their home in the San Francisco Peaks during the remainder of the year.

In the future, more will be learned about the development of Hopi religion through archaeological, historical, and ethnographic research. Perhaps we will discover that Hopi references to the Grand Canyon are metaphors of the earlier life and experiences of the Canyon Anasazi. But for the present, the little we know about the possible relationship between the fate of the Canyon Anasazi and the nature of Hopi religion stands as one more of the intriguing puzzles in our study of Grand Canyon prehistory.

Kiva ladder, Hopi pueblo. Photo from Emry Kopta Collection, courtesy Museum of Northern Arizona.

Chapter IX

The Grand Canyon, looking towards the North Rim. Photo by Peter Dechert, 1970.
School of American Research.

On The Edge of Splendor

The prehistory of the Grand Canyon is not an isolated chapter of the human adventure but part of the vast pageant that began when our species moved beyond the African heartland, eventually expanding to the farthest corners of the earth. At first, people spread to the best adjacent land, most like the country they had left behind, where they could employ familiar ways to make a living. As their numbers increased, they were forced to occupy less familiar and increasingly less desirable environments, adjusting by developing new tools and methods of survival.

Gradually, over the millennia, all the best lands were claimed, forcing some groups into remote mountain regions, the driest deserts, ice-bound peninsulas, tropical rain forests, and the deepest canyons. These spare lands, which held much less potential for leading a secure life, greatly challenged the ability of the new inhabitants to survive. Yet again and again, struggling against powerful odds, they learned the use of new plants, hunted over more and more difficult terrain, and devised ways of withstanding extremes of temperature, rainfall, and altitude. In the process, they inhabited a world.

This expansion into the earth's marginal regions was led by individuals of singular initiative and vision — the pioneers who throughout history have been the first to explore beyond their home-lands in search of a better way of life, preparing the way for others to follow. Each of the five prehistoric cultures of the Grand Canyon would have been preceded by their pioneers. Although we will never know their names or faces, these individuals (probably young males, judging from our knowledge of historic frontier expansion) played an impor-tant part in the beginnings of each successive episode of canyon settlement.

The scouts came first — men who knew the land from years of hunting expeditions. Most of the new settlements in the canyon, as in other episodes of human expansion throughout the world, came from nearby territories, not in dramatic migrations over great distances. Once they had determined that settlement was a reasonable gamble, the first families arrived. They would find water and begin the process of adapting to the new terrain and its resources, developing the techniques necessary to live off the land. Again judging from the experiences of historic pioneers, many of these lessons were learned slowly and painfully, with much fear and frequent failure.

These ancient people, who time and again moved into the canyon country, lived on the edge of splendor and desperation. When they first encountered the Grand Canyon, they, like us, may well have been awed by its magnificence. Yet the canyon's magnitude, which, with our civilized comforts, so nourishes our souls today, for them must have been just another obstacle to overcome. They probably had been pushed into the region by changes in their nearby homelands — a growing population, or changes in environment that made their life there more difficult — and were pulled by the prospect of mining the new land's potential.

At least five times over the past four thousand years, culturally distinct people entered the canyon's rugged landscape, hoping first to survive there and later creating a secure home. Yet eventually, except for the Havasupais, they were overwhelmed by some powerful ecological or cultural change and vanished from the scene forever.

First to arrive, the foraging Archaic people lasted far longer than any of the others, perhaps because their unspecialized and flexible culture could take advantage of the widest range of foods. Not unlike our Paleolithic ancestors, their population of small bands rose and fell as the environment offered more or fewer resources, much as animal species are reduced in number as food becomes scarce, only to rebound as the environment permits. Eventually, however, the Archaic people left the canyon country, perhaps when faced with some catastrophic ecological event.

The Paiutes, with a culture similar to that of the Archaic people, lasted only four to five hundred years. They may have survived many times longer until jolted by some biological shock if their society and traditional pattern of life had not been decimated by Western disease and settlement.

The farming Cohonina, Anasazi, and Havasupais were also less successful than the foragers of the Archaic period. The Cohonina, with their rudimentary agriculture, and the Anasazi, with a more fully developed farming life, also lived in the canyon region for little more than four hundred years, until both were overcome by the drought of the A.D. 1100s, which made agriculture impossible. All that remains of these two cultures are hundreds of archaeological sites and the Hopi legends that may reflect the life of their Canyon Anasazi ancestors.

The well-watered canyon home of the Havasupais, who were part-time farmers, shielded them from drought and partially protected them from the harsh impact of Western culture, which destroyed the Kaibab Paiutes. For a century, the impact of the American newcomers ate away at Havasupai land and culture, but with the return of a major part of their territory, the tide may now be turning. Although they have already lost much of their traditional culture, as long as Havasu Creek continues to flow they may continue to survive as an ethnic identity, the only resident Indian survivors with ties to the canyon's prehistory.

During their transitory settlement in the canyon region, each of these five cultures had to deal with similar universal human problems: explaining the unknown forces around them, educating their young, organizing their society, and finding meaning in life and death. The discovery of the Archaic figurines and the significance of the canyon sipapuni to the Hopis have given us some intriguing glimpses into the ritual life of these cultures. But the nature of archaeological research is such that we may never learn the details, for example, of their origin myths, their central value system, the techniques of their shamans, or their views of an afterlife. So while the people of these cultures may have collected the same kinds of berries, hunted the same species of animals, and quenched their thirst from the same springs, the meanings they gave to these actions, as varied as the richness of the human imagination, will always be lost to us.

Even with the great difference between the canyon cultures, widely separated in time, we know their lives were bound together by the gigantic divide of the Grand Canyon itself. From the vantage of our comfortable lives, we see canyons, deserts, mountains, and swamps as major environmental challenges, but for those of us who are raised among them, they are more often taken for granted. Anyone who has seen an apparently frail Indian woman climbing a steep mountainside carrying an impossibly heavy load of firewood can appreciate this distinction. Climbing into or out of the Grand Canyon may be a great adventure for us, and not without its hardships, but to those who lived there, the experience may have been an ordinary part of their lives. Therefore, we should be careful not to exaggerate the physical difficulties of the canyon in the life of these people.

During the early history of the Southwest, the Grand Canyon was a major obstruction to north-south travel, and we know it was necessary for the Spaniards and Americans to go great distances to circumvent its chasm. Even today, to get from the South Rim to the North Rim, it is necessary to drive around it — a distance of over three hundred miles. Therefore, it is logical for us to think that the canyon was also a forbidding physical barrier to prehistoric Indians, but the archaeological and ethnographic evidence suggests otherwise. Both the Archaic people and the Anasazi lived on either side of the river and appear to have moved from one side to the other and throughout the canyon without undue difficulty.

For other canyon people, the river may also have been less of an obstacle than a cultural marker. While the Cohonina lived mainly south of the river, for a time in the A.D. 900s they used some areas on the north side, indicating they could cross with some impunity. And although the Havasupais and the Kaibab Paiutes had complementary territories on the south and north sides of the river, they occasionally crossed into the other's land, suggesting the river was less an obstruction than the accepted line between them. Thus, over time the canyon may not have been the barrier to travel and expansion that we might envision, but a convenient cultural boundary between adjacent people.

Beyond its physical nature, the canyon must also have been of deep spiritual significance to its ancient inhabitants. We know the Hopis saw it as a place of special meaning and power — the origin of their ancestors, the source of sacred waters and salt, and the home of Maasaw. While next to nothing is known about how the canyon was perceived by the other prehistoric societies who lived there, it is reasonable that they too made it part of their ideology, responding with awe to its dimensions and colors, marveling that even in these arid surroundings, water always flowed at its deepest levels, or that it seemed to vanish when it filled with clouds.

It has been my good fortune to be deeply involved in piecing together the prehistory of the Grand Canyon — a much more complex story than I ever could have imagined when I began this venture so many years ago. When my work began, I thought I was just looking for prehistoric remains and trying to learn something about their nature. It never occurred to me that eventually, I would be considering the widespread pattern of pioneers searching for new lands; the problems and fears of early settlers; and the effects of a harsh environment, occupied in patches and intermittently over time, often leaving the inhabitants with little but the barest essentials of life. Through these studies, I have also learned great respect for the canyon's ancient inhabitants — a dimly perceived shaman, helping others to make sense of an uncertain world; and the waves of people who entered the canyon, each with its own ways of surviving, who were beaten back time and again by adverse conditions, only to return in another guise. Time and again, their struggles have led me to recognize the indomitable human will to endure.

Recently I was struck by a quotation from the philosopher George Santayana about the "intrinsic vitality" that comes from familiarity with old places and old people and how these provide longer perspectives and broader intellectual foundations. That kind of vitality is the gift that has come to me through my explorations of the Grand Canyon, tramping through time over its distant human landscapes, communing with ancient figurine makers, and joining all those who, over time, have traveled to the sipapuni. For me, this work has combined a search for the particular and the general, examining the human story of a uniquely awe-inspiring environment and helping to uncover something more about the complex nature of the human species.

The Grand Canyon. Photo by John MacGregor, 1968. School of American Research.

References

Chapter I

Muir, John. "The Wild Peaks and Forest Reservations of the West." *Atlantic Monthly*, Jan. 1898.

Schwartz, Douglas W. "A Historical Analysis and Synthesis of Grand Canyon Archaeology." *American Antiquity* 31, no. 4 (Apr. 1966): 469–84.

Chapter II

Goetzmann, William H. *Exploration and Empire: The Explorer and the Scientist in the Winning of the American West*. New York: W. W. Norton and Company, 1966.

Powell, John Wesley. *The Exploration of the Colorado River and Its Canyons*. New York: Dover, 1961.

Chapter III

Frazer, James. *The Golden Bough: A Study in Magic and Religion*. New York: Abelard-Schuman, 1956.

Schaafsma, Polly. "Shaman's Gallery: A Grand Canyon Rock Art Site. AZ B:9:201." Report for Grand Canyon National Park, 1988.

Schwartz, Douglas W., Arthur L. Lange, and Raymond deSaussure. "Split Twig Figurines in the Grand Canyon." *American Antiquity* 23, no. 3 (Jan. 1958): 264–74.

Chapter IV

Euler, Robert C. "Southern Paiute Archaeology." *American Antiquity* 29, no. 3 (Jan. 1964): 379–81.

Fowler, Don D., and Catherine S. Fowler. "The Ethnography of the Canyon Country." In *John Wesley Powell and the Anthropology of the Canyon Country*, pp. 20–28. Geological Survey Professional Paper 670. 1969.

Kelly, Isabel T. *Southern Paiute Ethnography*. Glen Canyon Series 21, University of Utah Anthropological Papers 69. Salt Lake City, 1964.

Kelly, Isabel T., and Catherine S. Fowler. "Southern Paiute." In *Handbook of North American Indians*. Vol. 11, *Great Basin*, edited by Warren L. D'Azevedo. Washington, D.C.: Smithsonian Institution, 1986.

Chapter V

Cartledge, Thomas R. "Cohonina Adaptation to the Colorado Plateau: A Re-Evaluation." *The Kiva* 44 (1979): 297–317.

Colton, Harold S. "Prehistoric Culture Units and Their Relationships in Northern Arizona." Museum of Northern Arizona Bulletin No. 17. Flagstaff, 1939.

Euler, Robert C. "Havasupai-Cohonina Relationships in the Grand Canyon." In *Collected Papers in Honor of Erik Kellerman Reed*, edited by Albert H. Schroeder, pp. 167–75. Anthropological Papers 6. Albuquerque: Archaeological Society of New Mexico Press, 1981.

Jennings, Calvin H. "Early Prehistory of the Coconino Plateau, Northwestern Arizona." Ph.D. diss., University of Colorado, 1971. Ann Arbor: University Microfilms.

McGregor, John C., and contributors. *The Cohonina Culture of Northwestern Arizona*. Urbana: University of Illinois Press, 1951.

Chapter VI

Hinton, Leanne. "Havasupai Songs: A Linguistic Perspective." Ph.D. diss., University of California, San Diego, 1977.

———."Vocables in Havasupai Song." In *Southwestern Indian Ritual Drama*, edited by Charlotte J. Frisbie, pp. 275–305. Albuquerque: University of New Mexico Press, 1980.

Schwartz, Douglas W. "Havasupai Prehistory: Thirteen Centuries of Cultural Development." Ph.D. diss., Yale University, 1955.

———."Havasupai." In *Handbook of North American Indians*, vol. 9, edited by Alfonso Ortiz. Washington: Smithsonian Institution, 1979.

Spier, Leslie. "Havasupai Ethnography." Anthropological Papers of the American Museum of Natural History, vol. 29, no. 3, pp. 83–292. New York: American Museum of Natural History, 1928.

Chapter VII

Dean, Jeffrey S., and William K. Robinson. *Dendroclimatic Variability in the American Southwest, A.D. 680 to 1970*. Report to the National Park Service.

Tucson: Laboratory of Tree-Ring Research, University of Arizona, 1977.

Effland, Richard W., A. Trinkle Jones, and Robert C. Euler. "The Archaeology of Powell Plateau: Regional Interaction at Grand Canyon." Grand Canyon Natural History Association Monograph 3. 1981.

Haury, Emil W. *Kivas of the Tusayan Ruin, Grand Canyon Arizona.* Medallion Papers No. 9. Globe, Arizona: Gila Pueblo, 1931.

Schwartz, Douglas W. "Archaeological Investigations in the Shinumo Area of Grand Canyon, Arizona." *Plateau* 32, no. 3 (Jan. 1960): 61–67.

———. "An Archaeological Survey of Nankoweap Canyon, Grand Canyon National Park." *American Antiquity* 28, no. 3 (Jan. 1963): 289–302.

———. "Nankoweap to Unkar: An Archaeological Survey of the Upper Grand Canyon." *American Antiquity* 30, no. 3 (Jan. 1965): 278–96.

Schwartz, Douglas W., Michael P. Marshall, and Jane Kepp. *Archaeology of the Grand Canyon: The Bright Angel Site.* Grand Canyon Archaeology Series, vol. 1. Santa Fe: School of American Research Press, 1979.

Schwartz, Douglas W., Richard C. Chapman, and Jane Kepp. *Archaeology of the Grand Canyon: Unkar Delta.* Grand Canyon Archaeology Series, vol. 2. Santa Fe: School of American Research Press, 1980.

———. *Archaeology of the Grand Canyon: The Walhalla Plateau.* Grand Canyon Archaeology Series, vol. 3. Santa Fe: School of American Research Press, 1981.

Sullivan, Alan P., Owen K. Davis, Robert W. Layhe, Linda Scott, L. Keiko Yoshikawa, and Barbara A. Murphy. *Prehistory of the Upper Basin, Coconino County, Arizona.* Archaeological Series No. 167. Tucson: Cultural Resource Management Division, Arizona State Museum, University of Arizona, 1986.

Chapter VIII

Eggan, Fred. "The Hopi Indians, with Special Reference to Their Cosmology or World View, As Expressed in Their Traditions, Religious Beliefs, Practices and Social Organization." Ms. from the author, 1986.

Frisbie, Charlotte J., ed. *Southwestern Indian Ritual Drama.* Albuquerque: University of New Mexico Press, 1980.

Malotki, Ekkehart, and Michael Lomatuway'ma. *Hopi Coyote Tales — Istutuwutsi.* Vol. 9 of *American Tribal Religions.* Lincoln and London: University of Nebraska Press, 1984.

Talayesva, Don C. *Sun Chief: The Autobiography of a Hopi Indian.* New Haven: Yale University Press, 1942.

Voth, Henry R. "Four Hopi Tales." In *Brief Hopi Miscellaneous Papers.* Anthropological Series No. 157. Chicago: Field Columbian Museum, 1912.

Whiteley, Peter. *Bacavi: Journey to Reed Springs.* Flagstaff: Northland Press, 1988.

The School of American Research

 The School of American Research is a unique center for anthropological studies, founded in 1907 in Santa Fe, New Mexico. The School is committed to seeking new ideas and insights that contribute to a better understanding of the human species. In pursuit of this goal, we support scholars whose research and writing explore the human experience and provide us with a meaningful sense of our shared humanity.

The School supports resident scholars, conducts week-long seminars for professional anthropologists, sponsors research on its extensive Southwest Indian art collections, publishes innovative books in the field of anthropology, and offers a major book award. Our campus offers a beautiful, quiet environment for scholars to study and write.

We would welcome you as a member of the School. By joining, you will receive our newsletters and annual report, future issues of *Exploration*, and a discount on our books. You will also have an opportunity to join various membership activities. And you will play a part in supporting our professional activities.

For more information on the School of American Research, please contact the membership office at Post Office Box 2188, Santa Fe, New Mexico 87504-2188, or call (505) 984-0742.